THE WORLD
UCL
1828 - 1990

First edition 1978
Revised edition 1991

Published by UCL
Gower Street
London WC1E 6BT

© University College London 1991

ISBN 0-902137-32-8 (hbk.)
ISBN 0-902137-31-X (pbk.)

A CIP catalogue record for this book
is available from the British Library.

Designed and produced for UCL by
Newpoint Consultancy Services
Windsor Court
East Grinstead House
East Grinstead
West Sussex RH19 1XA

A Reed International Company

Designed by Phil Bushell
Typeset by AVS Ltd
Printed in Great Britain
by Biddles Ltd

THE WORLD OF
UCL
1828 - 1990

EST FRONT.

NIVERSITY OF LONDON

NEGLEY HARTE AND JOHN NORTH

Foreword by
DR DEREK ROBERTS CBE FRS FEng
PROVOST

FOREWORD

In his introduction to the first edition of this book, Lord Annan noted that in some ways 'College' is a misnomer for UCL. 'For that word', he wrote, 'carries with it the overtones of a cosy inward-looking society, somewhat complacent, inevitably preoccupied with preserving hoary rituals and enhancing the beauty of exquisite lawns and buildings, perhaps a little too ready to put the interests of community life before the duty to further the acquisition of wisdom and learning. University College is nothing if not austere. When its members recount its history they see it in terms of the great "Profs". Everything centres upon the department and its record of research'. This book certainly brings out UCL's record of research and its great professors, and it shows that the world of UCL is fascinating in all sorts of ways. But it is not only its past which is interesting.

This revision of *The World of UCL* embraces the period of Sir James Lighthill's Provostship between 1979 and 1989. It was a period made difficult by continuous cuts in university funding by the UGC – but it was also a period of very successful academic change and expansion for UCL. This was brought about by the creation of the University College and Middlesex School of Medicine and the incorporation of the Institute of Archaeology into UCL, coupled with a major increase in research activity based on funds from Research Councils, UK Charities and Industry and the European Community.

Expansion has no justification if it is at the expense of quality – but this was not a problem under Sir James's leadership. Two successive reviews by the UGC of research quality in UK universities placed UCL firmly in the top three multi-faculty institutions in the country. This achievement, coupled with such other events as the attractions of the Sandoz laboratories and the Ludwig Institute to UCL – to say nothing of raising the funds for completing the Gower Street frontage – was achieved in spite of the Establishment. But then, what is new? The founders of UCL in the 1820s had similar experiences.

Change and growth coupled with academic excellence continue. This is illustrated by success in attracting Research Councils' funds for the creation of Interdisciplinary Research Centres; the commitment to three new buildings on the Gordon Street/South Junction site to house respectively the Advanced centre for Biochemical Engineering; the Eisai Research Laboratory for Molecular Biology and the MRC-funded IRC in Cell Biology. The Arts also have their successes with the acquisition of the old Courtauld Gallery building for the Slade's postgraduate painting studios. The acquisition of the H. K. Lewis bookshop, as an integral part of the Gower Street rectangle, now being devoted to a new language centre and expansion of our Economics Department's activities in Economic Research in the Global Environment is another significant advance. Within the Institute of Archaeology the creation of the 'Wolfson Archaeological Science Laboratories' builds a new and important link between science and the humanities.

Lest it should be considered that attention is so concentrated on research that our undergraduates are ignored, it should also be noted that throughout the Lighthill years there has been a commitment, which continues, to the expansion of student residential accommodation and of the UCL Union facilities.

The founders of UCL could easily have adopted as their theme 'Equal Opportunities'. That is another continuing area of success for UCL relative to UK academe in general with, for example, a ratio of female to male professors which is over three times better than the national average.

The achievements of the past must of course never be allowed to create a complacent attitude. Much remains to be achieved – and will be. But that story must await the next revision of *The World of UCL*.

D. H. Roberts.

Provost

1. An aerial view from above Euston station taken in 1990 of UCL showing the whole of the 'rectangle' site, with University College Hospital and the Medical School buildings beyond, and Wates House, the Department of Chemistry and the Institute of Archaeology in the foreground. In the centre is the main building which was opened as the 'University of London' in October 1828, the architect's original design for which is shown on the title-page.

2

It is generally but wrongly believed that Jeremy Bentham was the founder of University College London. This myth is sustained in a bizarre manner by the display of the body of the great philosopher of ethics, jurisprudence and government, 'in the attitude', as he himself instructed before his death in 1832, 'in which I am sitting when engaged in thought'. The 'Auto-Icon' has been in the possession of the College since 1850.

Besides the box with Bentham in it, the College possesses over 200 more boxes full of his writings, a collection that has been called 'one of the most remarkable monuments to the mind of a single man in all its aspects to be found anywhere'. Prominently displayed in the Flaxman Gallery, moreover, is the huge painting undertaken in 1922 by Henry Tonks, the then Slade Professor of Fine Art, portraying William Wilkins, the architect, offering the original College plans up to Bentham for his approval, while Henry Brougham, Thomas Campbell and Crabb Robinson look on.

In fact Bentham played no such close personal role in the establishment of the College. When the College first opened its doors to students as the self-styled 'University of London' in October 1828, Bentham was an old withdrawn man of 80. He gave his blessing and financial support to the moves to found a university in the largest city in Europe and the only capital without one, and the founders certainly owed a very considerable intellectual debt to him.

Since 1959 the Bentham Project, based in the College, has been engaged on the massive enterprise of preparing for publication Bentham's collected works and correspondence; sixteen volumes have appeared so far, and over fifty more are planned. The 'Auto-Icon' attended the sesquicentennial meeting of the College Committee in 1976, the minutes recording 'Jeremy Bentham present but not voting'.

2. Henry Tonks's remarkable but completely unhistorical painting of the building of the College, showing William Wilkins offering his plans up to Jeremy Bentham for approval.

3. An extraordinary possession of the College is the clothed skeleton of Jeremy Bentham, as displayed with a wax head, in its box in the South Cloisters.

4. An even more extraordinary possession is Bentham's actual mummified head, now kept in the College safe.

3.

4.

The College was founded by what Bentham called 'an association of liberals', a description he used in a recently-discovered letter written in August 1825 to Bolivar, the South American liberator. The leading roles were played by an improbable duo formed by a poet and a lawyer.

Credit for the original proposal must go to Thomas Campbell, the now forgotten Scottish poet whose *Pleasures of Hope* (1799) brought him popular fame and a rapid entrée into London literary society. In 1820, on a visit to Bonn, he was impressed by the religious toleration of the re-founded university there and formed the idea of establishing 'a great London University' for 'effectively and multifariously teaching, examining, exercising and rewarding with honours, in the liberal arts and sciences, the youth of our middling rich people...' In February 1825 *The Times* printed a powerful open letter on this subject from Campbell to

Henry Brougham, another Scot, a brilliant man, one of the founders of the *Edinburgh Review*, who had moved to London to seek commanding outlets in the law and in politics for his versatility and energy. An MP first in 1810, he became particularly involved with the cause of popular education, associating himself with George Birkbeck and the mechanics' institutes and founding in 1826 the Society for the Diffusion of Useful Knowledge, the papers of which are now in the College Library, as are Brougham's own papers.

Brougham regarded himself as a Benthamite, as a believer in the utilitarian principle of 'the greatest happiness of the greatest number' – though it has been claimed that in his view the greatest number was number one. His extravagant style smacked of humbug to many, but he was a man who got things done. Under his direction, Campbell's dreams for a London University were turned into reality.

5. The first of the effective founders of the College, the poet Thomas Campbell (1777-1844), an engraving based on his portrait by Sir Thomas Lawrence.

6. The second and even more effective of the founders of the College, the lawyer and politician Henry Brougham FRS MP (1778-1868), after 1830 Lord Brougham and Vaux, as painted by James Lonsdale.

5.

6.

7. The University of Bonn as it appeared when visited by Campbell in 1820.

8. A second university which provided a model for the new university in London was Jefferson's carefully planned University of Virginia, seen here soon after its opening in 1825.

9. The University of Edinburgh was the most powerful model of all, familiar as it was to Brougham and many of the founding professoriate in London.

by Tho. H. Shepherd   Engraved W. H. I

THE UNIVERSITY, SOUTH BRIDGE STREET,

11.

10.

COUNCIL
HON. JAMES ABERCROMBIE M.P.
RIGHT HON LORD AUCKLAND.
ALEXANDER BARING ESQ. M.P.
GEORGE BIRKBECK M.D.
HENRY BROUGHAM ESQ. M.P. F.R.S.
THOMAS CAMPBELL ESQ.
RIGHT HON. VISCOUNT DUDLEY AND WARD
ISAAC LYON GOLDSMID ESQ.
OLINTHUS G. GREGORY LL.D.
GEORGE GROTE JUN ESQ.
JOSEPH HUME ESQ. M.P. F.R.S.
MOST NOBLE THE MARQUIS OF LANSDOWNE F.R.E
ZACHARY MACAULAY ESQ. F.R.S.
SIR JAMES MACKINTOSH M.P. F.R.S.
JAMES MILL ESQ.
HIS GRACE THE DUKE OF NORFOLK.
LORD JOHN RUSSELL M.P.
BENJAMIN SHAW ESQ.
JOHN SMITH ESQ. M.P.
WILLIAM TOOKE ESQ. F.R.S.
HENRY WARBURTON ESQ. F.R.S.
HENRY WAYMOUTH ESQ.
JOHN WHISHAW ESQ. F.R.S.
THOMAS WILSON ESQ.

10. The foundation medal recording the names of the original Council.

11. The portrait of one of the leading members, Sir Isaac Lyon Goldsmid, presented to the College by the Jewish Historical Society of England.

When Campbell and Brougham began to organise a university for London, the only existing universities in England were those long established at Oxford and Cambridge – 'the two great public nuisances', Bentham called them, 'storehouses and nurseries of political corruption...' Membership of the Church of England was necessary for admission to the one and for graduation from the other. All nonconformists, Catholics and Jews were thus excluded, while many Anglicans were kept out by the social restrictiveness, by the cost or by the characteristic intellectual backwardness. The old universities were seen to be increasingly out of touch with a rapidly changing society. The population doubled in the first half of the nineteenth century and the combined effects of industrialisation and of urbanisation were making for new social patterns with new pressures and new demands. The industrial revolution necessitated an extended system of higher education.

The main appeal of the new university was therefore to the interests excluded from the established system, such as it was, and to the various new social groups. Isaac Lyon Goldsmid, a millionaire financier and later to be the first Jew to become a baronet, played an especially significant role. He it was who brought Campbell and Brougham together on the project and he ensured the considerable support of the Jewish community. The nonconformists were actively led by Francis Augustus Cox, the Baptist minister of Hackney, while a different dissenting strand was represented by the support of Zachary Macaulay, whose main work had been devoted to the abolition of the slave trade. The Catholics were represented by the Duke of Norfolk, and the Whig establishment provided a number of other titled luminaries. James Mill, the utilitarian philosopher, actively represented Benthamism, and the various progressive influences rubbed shoulders readily with supporters from the City.

among your friends with a view to an early
'ainment of the important objects of the Institution.
We have the honor to be

London,
20th March 1826

Your most obedient Servants

J. Abercrombie.
Auckland
Alexr Baring
George Birkbeck
H Brougham
Thos Campbell
Dudley & Ward
Isaac Lyon Goldsmid
Olinthus Gregory
Geo. Grote
Joseph Hume
Lansdowne
T. Macaulay
J J Mackintosh
J Mill
Norfolk
Russell
B. Shaw
John Smith.
Wm Tooke
Henry Warburton
R. Waymouth
J. Whishaw
Thomas Wilson

All communications on the subject of subscriptions or otherwise
to be addressed to "Wm Coates" (Clerk to the Council)
"No 4 Furnivals Inn."

12. The signatures of all the
twenty-four members of the
original Council.

13. James Mill.

14. Zachary Macaulay.

15. George Grote.

16. George Birkbeck.

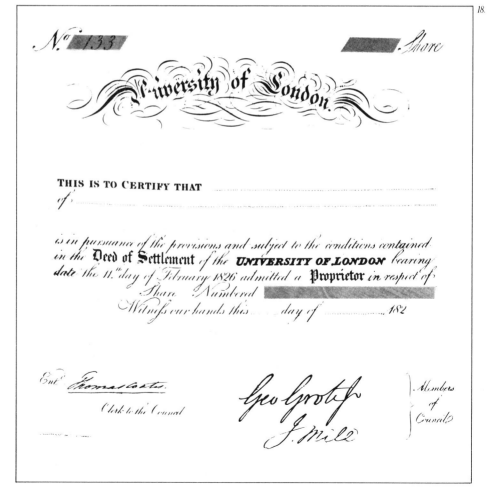

As the result of a year-long series of meetings both public and private chaired by Brougham, the College came into formal existence on 11 February 1826 with the signing of an elaborate Deed of Settlement. It was agreed to raise a substantial sum of between £150,000 and £300,000 by the selling of shares of £100 each. From among the 'proprietors', as the shareholders were called, twenty-four persons were to be elected as the Council, the all-powerful body which was to control the University's property, appoint the professors and regulate the education of the students. It was a fundamental principle of the new institution that religion in any form should be neither a requirement for entry, nor a subject for teaching. As a corollary it was decided that no minister of religion should sit on the Council. The Revd Dr Cox served therefore as Honorary Secretary of that body until becoming Librarian in 1827.

17. The bust of the Revd Dr Francis Augustus Cox which remains in the room of his successor as Librarian.

18. One of the share certificates as issued to the original proprietors.

19. Cruikshank's cartoon of Brougham hawking shares in the projected University around Lincoln's Inn.

Nᵒ 133 Share

University of London.

THIS IS TO CERTIFY THAT

of

is in pursuance of the provisions and subject to the conditions contained in the **Deed of Settlement** of the **UNIVERSITY OF LONDON** bearing date the 11.ᵗʰ day of February 1826 admitted a **Proprietor** in respect of Share Numbered
Witness our hands this day of 182

Ent.ᵈ Thomas Coates
Clerk to the Council

Geo Grote
J. Mill

Members of Council

The POLITICAL, TOY-MAN.

21.

20.

From the outset the promoters sought incorporation. Brougham's soundings towards a royal charter in 1825 were rebuffed by the Tory government of the day, and his subsequent efforts to achieve an Act of Parliament were defeated by the influence of Oxford and Cambridge. Parliamentary assistance was provided by Joseph Hume, one of the members of the original Council, a leading radical who was indefatigable in support of the College as well as of those other great progressive causes of the age, catholic emancipation and parliamentary reform. After 1832 he was joined in the House of Commons by another member of the original Council, William Tooke, a prominent solicitor who became the first Treasurer of the College and of the Hospital. The strength of the combined opposition of Oxbridge and of the London medical profession to legal recognition of the College as a 'University' could not easily be overcome in Parliament, despite the efforts also of Brougham in the House of Lords, where he had astonishingly gone in 1830 as Lord Chancellor. When the College did eventually get its first charter in 1836, it took an unexpected form.

UNIVERSITY OF LONDON.

PROSPECTUS.

The Plan of the University of London is now so much matured, that the Council, chosen to superintend its affairs, deem themselves bound to lay an outline of it before the public, in order that the friends of public instruction may have the fullest opportunity of determining how far the Institution deserves their support, and of considering in what particulars it may seem to them capable of improvement.

The number and names of the Subscribers sufficiently evince the strong conviction of its utility which prevails in the class of men for whom the Institution is peculiarly destined, and who consult their own interest, as well as that of the public, in contributing towards its establishment.

The City of London is nearly equal in population, and far superior in wealth, to each of the Kingdoms of Denmark, Saxony, Hanover, and Wirtemburgh, every one of which has at least one flourishing University. Supposing the annual rate of increase, in the last five years, to have been the same as in the preceding ten, the present population cannot be less than fourteen hundred thousand souls,* of whom there are about forty thousand males, between the ages of sixteen and twenty-one ; the usual period of academical education. It may safely be affirmed, that there is no equal number of youths in any other place, of whom so large a portion feel the want of liberal education, are so well qualified for it, could so easily obtain all its advantages at home, and are so little able to go in quest of them elsewhere. No where else is knowledge more an object of desire, either as a source of gratification, a means of improvement, or an instrument of honest and useful ambition. The exclusion of so great a body of intelligent youth, designed for the most important occupations in society, from the highest means of liberal education, is a defect in our institutions, which, if it were not become familiar by its long prevalence, would offend every reasonable mind. In a word, London, which, for intelligence and wealth, as well as numbers, may fairly be deemed the first City in the civilized world, is at once the place which most needs an University, and the only great Capital which has none.

Public Lectures, combined with examinations by the Professors, and with mutual instruction by the pupils, will form the general system of this Institution. It is intended, that the Professors shall derive their income at first principally, and, as soon as may be, entirely, from the fees paid by their pupils ; and they will hold their offices during good behaviour. We are assured, that Professors will be found of eminent ability, and of such established reputation, as to give authority and lustre to their instructions, so that the University will not be wanting in the means of exciting and guiding superior faculties in their ascent to excellence, as well as of speedily and easily imparting the needful share of knowledge to all diligent students. The number of the Professors, the allotment of particular branches to individuals, and the order in which the Lectures ought to be attended, are matters not yet finally settled, and some of them must partly depend, in the first instance, on the qualifications of candidates ; all of them will permanently be regulated by the demand for different sorts of instruction. Some Professorships may hereafter be consolidated ; more are likely, in process of time to be subdivided ; many entirely new will doubtless be rendered necessary by the progress of discovery, and by the enlarged desire of the community for knowledge. The Course of Instruction will at present consist of Languages, Mathematics, Physics, the Mental and the Moral Sciences, together with the Law of England, History, and Political Economy ;—and the various branches of knowledge which are the objects of Medical Education. In the classification of these studies there is no intention to adhere strictly to a logical order, whether founded upon the subjects to which each relates, or on the faculties principally employed on it. Without entirely losing sight of these considerations, our main guide is the convenience of teaching, which for the present purpose is more important than a scientific arrangement ; even if such an arrangement could be well made without a new nomenclature of the sciences, and a new distribution of their objects.

Some Languages will probably be studied only by those whose peculiar destination requires such attainments, and in this department generally, it will be fit to seek for every method of abridging the labour by which the majority are to attain that proficiency to which they ought to confine themselves. But the structure of human speech is itself one of the worthiest objects of meditation : the comparison of various languages, makes each of them better understood, and illustrates the affinity of nations, while it enlarges and strengthens every vigorous understanding ; even the minute and seemingly unfruitful study of words is a school of discrimination and precision ; and in the arts which employ language as their instrument, the contemplation of the original models, not only serves to form the taste of the youth of genius, but generally conduces to expand and elevate the human faculties.

The Mathematical Sciences are so justly valued as a discipline of the reasoning faculties, and as an unerring measure of human advancement, that the commendation of them might seem disrespectful to the judgment of the reader, if they did not afford by far the most striking instance of the dependance of the most common and useful arts upon abstruse reasoning. The elementary propositions of Geometry were once merely speculative ; but those to whom their subserviency to the speed and safety of voyages, is now familiar, will be slow to disparage any truth for the want of present and palpable usefulness.

It is a matter of considerable difficulty to ascertain the distribution of Physics, a vast science, or rather class of sciences, which consists in the knowledge of the most general facts observed by the senses in the things without us. Some of these appearances are the subject of calculation, and must, in teaching, be blended with the Mathematics ; others are chiefly discovered and proved by experiment ; one portion of physical observation relates to the movements of conspicuous masses, while another relates to the reciprocal action of the imperceptible particles or agents which we know only by their results ; and a great part are founded on that uniformity of structure, and those important peculiarities of action, which distinguish vegetable and animal life. The subjoined division of professorships in this province, though chiefly adapted to the practical purpose of instruction, is influenced by some regard to the above considerations.

* By the returns of 1821, the numbers were 1,274,000.

20. William Tooke FRS, an engraving published in the Illustrated London News after his death in 1863: one of the members of the original Council who as a radical MP fought for full recognition and incorporation for the College.

21. Joseph Hume FRS, as painted by John Lucas in the largest portrait on display in the College: another member of the original Council who was a radical MP.

22. The following three pages: the Prospectus produced by the original Council of February 1826 laying out in some detail the scheme of education to be offered.

22.

As the Physical Sciences aim at ascertaining the most general facts observed by sense in the things which are the objects of thought, so the MENTAL SCIENCES seek to determine the most general facts as relating to thought or feelings, made known to the being who thinks, by his own consciousness.

The sub-division of this part of knowledge, would be very desirable on account of its importance and intricacy; but the close connexion of all the facts with each other renders it peculiarly difficult.

A separate Professorship of LOGIC is proposed, not only because it supplies the rules of argument, and the tests of sophistry, but still more for that mental regimen by which it slowly dispels prejudice and strengthens habits of right judgment.

Perhaps, also, RHETORIC, or the Art of Persuasion, may in time merit a separate Professorship, of which one main object would be to undeceive those rigid censurers, and misguided admirers, who consider it as a gaudy pageant; and to imbue the minds of youth with the wholesome assurance that when guided by morality, and subjected to logic, it is the art of rendering truth popular, and virtue delightful; of transforming conviction into persuasion; and of engaging the whole man, the feelings as well as the understanding, on the side of true wisdom.

The object common to the MORAL SCIENCES, is the determination of the rules which ought to direct the voluntary actions of men; and they have generally been subdivided into Ethics and Jurisprudence; though the important distinction between these sciences has seldom been accurately traced, still less steadily observed. The direct object of Ethics is the knowledge of those habitual dispositions of mind which we approve as moral, or disapprove as immoral, and from which beneficial or mischievous actions ordinarily flow. Particular actions themselves are estimated by the motives from which they arise. Ethics is co-extensive with the whole character and conduct of man; it is the science of virtues and duties; of those dispositions which are praiseworthy, and of that course of action which is incumbent on a reasonable being, apart from the consideration of the injunctions of law, and the authority of civil government.

The first object of JURISPRUDENCE, (taking that term in an enlarged sense,) is the ascertainment of rights, or of those portions of power over persons or things which should be allotted to each individual for the general welfare. The second is to determine what violations of these rights are so injurious in their effects and consequences to society, as to require prevention by the fear of adequate punishment. It is the science of rights and of crimes; it pre-supposes the authority of government, and is limited in its direct operation to the outward actions of men as they affect each other. Ethics, though it has a wider scope, contemplates its objects more simply and generally. Jurisprudence, within its more limited sphere, considers its objects in more points of view; prescribes more exact rules, and is therefore compelled to make minute and even subtle distinctions. The confusion of these two branches of Moral Science has contributed to disturb the Theory of Ethics, and to corrupt the practice of legislation.

The study of the LAWS OF ENGLAND has for centuries been confined to the Capital, where alone there is a constant opportunity of observing its administration in Courts of Justice, and of acquiring skill in peculiar branches under private instructors. These exclusive advantages of London for the Study of the Law would surely be enhanced by combination with Lectures and Examinations, while systematic instruction in Law, and in general knowledge, would be rendered accessible to those branches of the legal profession which are now shut out from them by the impediments common to them with the Youth of the Metropolis in general.

The maxims which ought to be observed by independent communities towards each other, and of which the fitness is generally acknowledged by civilized states, constitute what is metaphorically called the LAW OF NATIONS.

POLITICAL PHILOSOPHY, which considers what are the rights and duties of Rulers and Subjects in relation to each other, may be conveniently taught by the Professor of Ethics.

In an arrangement which does not affect a rigid method, History and Political Economy may be classed either as parts or appendages of Moral Science. A minute knowledge of HISTORY cannot be communicated by Lectures. But the outline of General History, directions to the Student for historical reading, the subsidiary sciences of Geography and Chronology, together with some information respecting Numismatics and Diplomatics, and the rules of Historical Criticism will furnish ample scope for one Professor.

The science of POLITICAL ECONOMY seeks to ascertain the laws which regulate the production, distribution, and consumption of wealth, or the outward things obtained by labour, and needed or desired by men. It is now too justly valued to require any other remark, than that the occasional difficulty of applying its principles, and the differences of opinion to which that difficulty has given rise, form new reasons for the diligent cultivation of a science which is so indispensible to the well being of communities, and of which, as it depends wholly on facts, all the perplexities must be finally removed by accurate observation and precise language.

For the studies which are necessary in all the branches of the PROFESSION of MEDICINE, the greatest city of Europe possesses peculiar and inestimable advantages. It is in large towns only that a Medical School can exist. The means of acquiring anatomical knowledge, medical experience, and surgical dexterity, must increase in exact proportion to the size of the town. At this moment the great majority of those who are called general practitioners, who take no degree, confine themselves to no single branch of the profession; but in whose hands the whole ordinary practice of England is placed, receive their systematic instruction from Lectures in London, for one or two years, while many of them attend hospitals. Their annual average is about seven hundred. Many of the Lecturers have been, and are men of very eminent ability; and the body of practitioners thus educated are, doubtless, very respectable for information and skill. It is no reflexion on either, to affirm, that Medical Education would be improved if the teachers of most distinguished ability who are now scattered over London, were gradually attracted to one Institution, where they would be stimulated to the utmost exertion of their faculties, by closer rivalship, larger emolument, and wider reputation. To what cause but to the present dispersion of eminent teachers can it be ascribed, that the greatest city of the civilized world is not its first School of Medicine?

The young men who are intended for the scientific profession of a CIVIL ENGINEER, which has of late been raised so high by men of genius, and exercised with such signal advantage to the public, have almost as strong reasons as those who are destined for the practice of Medicine, for desiring that a System of Academical Education should be accessible to them in the City, where alone they can be trained to skill and expertness under Artists of the first class.

The Council are rather encouraged than disheartened by the consideration that their undertaking rests on the voluntary contributions of individuals, on which, after the experience of a season of public difficulty, they now rely with firmer assurance. They are satisfied, that experience of its advantages will, in due time, procure for it such legal privileges as may be found convenient for its administration. For the good effects expected in other Seminaries from discipline, the Council put their trust in the power of Home and the care of Parents: to whom, in this Institution, which is equally open to the youth of every religious persuasion, the important duty of religious education is necessarily, as well as naturally left. That care, always the best wherever it can be obtained, will assuredly be adequate to every purpose in the case of the Residents in London, who must at first be the main foundation of the Establishment. When its reputation attracts many Pupils from the Country and the Colonies, the houses of Professors may afford those means of private instruction, and domestic superintendence, which have been found in other places to be excellent substitutes for parental care, and in the conduct of which the most justly celebrated men of this age have not disdained to take a part. They are not unwilling that the value of testimonials of proficiency and conduct, granted by the University, should, at least for the present, depend on the opinion entertained by the Public, of the judgment, knowledge, vigilance, and integrity, of the Professors.

Finally. The Council trust, that they are now about to lay the Foundation of an Institution well adapted to communicate liberal instruction to successive generations of those who are now excluded from it, and likely neither to retain the machinery of studies superseded by time, nor to neglect any new science brought into view by the progress of reason; of such magnitude as to combine the illustration and ornament which every part of knowledge derives from the neighbourhood of every other, with the advantage which accrues to all from the outward aids and instruments of Libraries, Museums, and Apparatus; where there will be a sufficient prospect of fame and emolument to satisfy the ambiton, and employ the whole active lives of the ablest Professors; which may thus contribute to restore the most eminent places in Education to their natural rank among the ultimate and highest objects of pursuit; where the least remission of diligence must give instant warning of danger, and an attempt to pervert its resources to personal purposes cannot fail to cut off the supply sought to be perverted; where the inseparable connexion of ample income, and splendid reputation with the general belief of meritorious service, may prove at once a permanent security for the ability of the Teachers, an incentive to their constant activity, and a preservative of the Establishment from decay.

I. LANGUAGE.

1. Greek Language, Literature, and Antiquities.
2. Roman Language, Literature, and Antiquities.
3. English Literature and Composition.
4. Oriental Literature, subdivided into,—
   A. Languages from the Mediterranean to the Indus.
   B. Languages from the Indus to the Burrampooter.
5. French Language and Literature.
6. Italian and Spanish Literature.
7. German and Northern Literature.

II. MATHEMATICS.

8. Elementary Mathematics.
9. Higher Mathematics.

III. HISTORY.

10. History.

IV. PHYSICS.

11. Mathematical Physics.
12. Experimental Physics
13. Chemistry.
14. Geology and Mineralogy.
15. Botany and Vegetable Physiology.
16. Zoology and Comparative Anatomy.
17. Application of Physical Sciences to the Arts.

V. MENTAL SCIENCE.

18. Philosophy of the Human Mind.
19. Logic.

VI. MORAL SCIENCES.

20. Moral and Political Philosophy.
21. Jurisprudence, including International Law.
22. English Law, with (perhaps) separate Lectures on the Constitution.
23. Roman Law.

VII. POLITICAL ECONOMY.

24. Political Economy.

VIII. MEDICAL SCIENCES.

25. Anatomy.
26. Physiology.
27. Surgery.
28. Midwifery and Diseases of Women and Children.
29. Materia Medica and Pharmacy.
30. Nature and Treatment of Diseases, together with
31. Clinical Lectures as soon as an Hospital can be connected with this Establishment.

(Signed, by Order of the Council,)

THOMAS COATES.

It is due to the Promoters of this Institution, to state the privileges and advantages to which they will be entitled in respect of their contributions, whether by subscription or donation to its funds.

The Deed of Settlement, fully provides for the protection of the Proprietors from all liability beyond the amount of the sums respectively subscribed by them. While it confers large powers on the Council, it also interposes every proper check on any irregularity in the exercise of those powers by the appointment of Auditors, and by General and Special Meetings of Proprietors for the revision of the proceedings of the Council and the adoption of such new By-Laws and Regulations as in the progress of the Establishment may from time to time be required.

The rights and privileges of the Proprietors under such Deed may thus shortly be recapitulated ;—

1. Absolute right of presentation of one Student, in respect of each Share, at such reduced rate of annual payment, and subject to such rules and restrictions as may be prescribed by the Council.
2. Interest on Shares not exceeding £4 per cent out of surplus income, (if any.)
3. Privilege of Transfer and Bequest of Shares.
4. In cases of Ballot, a Proprietor of one Share is entitled to one vote; of five Shares, to two votes; and of ten Shares, or upwards, to three votes, with privilege of voting by proxy at Elections.

Donors of £50 and upwards are entitled to all the privileges and advantages of Proprietors except as regards the transfer and devolution of their interest, and have no more than one vote on any occasion.

In addition, Proprietors and Donors will have the right of personal admission to the Library, and the various Collections of the University.

One of the first acquisitions for the College, even before it was officially constituted, was a building site. Nearly eight acres in Bloomsbury were bought in August 1825 for £30,000 by three of the richest promoters, Goldsmid, John Smith and Benjamin Shaw, and held by them until it could be transferred to the new University. Previously the site had served variously as a drilling ground, a place for duelling and as a rubbish dump. It had been intended to develop it as Carmarthen Square, a projected addition to the yet unfinished Bloomsbury.

24.

By the time of the holding of the first meeting of the proprietors at the end of October 1826, 1,300 shares in the University had been sold, 200 fewer than the minimum believed necessary. Plans for the building were nevertheless being pressed ahead, and the foundations were already being dug. Despite the bad weather of the winter of 1826-27 work was sufficiently advanced by 30 April 1827 for the ceremony of laying the foundation stone. This was undertaken with full masonic rights by the brother of the George IV, the Duke of Sussex, the only member of the royal family with any intellectual pretensions, well-known for his liberal sympathies. A copper plate with an inscription duly read out by Cox was placed in a cavity in the stone together with the traditional coins. Afterwards some 500 people gathered for a dinner at the Freemasons' Tavern at which many speeches were made, many healths drunk and £8,000 raised. Brougham made a memorably sarcastic oration attacking the opponents of the University, but annoyed Campbell's friends by appearing to accept credit for founding the University single-handed. Campbell was absent from the foundation ceremony being occupied as Lord Rector of the University of Glasgow and he did not serve on the Council beyond the first year. Squeezed out by Brougham, Campbell's connection with the University he proposed ended as it was coming into being.

25.

25. A plan of the projected Carmarthen Square development dated December 1824, before the site was acquired for the College.

26.

26. An invitation to the foundation ceremony for the College on 30 April 1827.

27. The Duke of Sussex, who laid the foundation stone, as painted by Guy Head.

27.

22

№ 25

DEO · OPT · MAX ·
SEMPITERNO · ORBIS · ARCHITECTO ·
FAVENTE ·
QVOD · FELIX · FAVSTVM · QVE · SIT ·
OCTAVVM · REGNI · ANNVM · INEVNTE ·
GEORGIO · QVARTO · BRITANNIARVM ·
REGE ·
CELSISSIMVS · PRINCEPS · AVGVSTVS · FREDERICVS ·
SUSSEXIAE · DVX ·
OMNIVM · BONARVM · ARTIVM · PATRONVS ·
ANTIQVISSIMI · ORDINIS · ARCHITECTONICI ·
PRAESES · APVD · ANGLOS · SVMMVS ·
PRIMVM · LONDINENSIS · ACADEMIAE · LAPIDEM ·
INTER · CIVIVM · ET · FRATRVM ·
CIRCVMSTANTIVM · PLAVSVS ·
MANV · SVA · LOCAVIT ·
PRID · KAL · MAII ·

OPVS ·
DIV · MVLTVM · QVE · DESIDERATVM ·
VRBI · PATRIAE · COMMODISSIMVM ·
TANDEM · ALIQVANDO · INCHOATVM · EST ·
ANNO · SALVTIS · HVMANAE ·
M · D · C · C · C · X · X · V · I · I ·
ANNO · LVCIS · NOSTRAE ·
M · M · M · M · M · D · C · C · C · X · X · V · I · I ·
NOMINA · CLARISSIMORVM · VIRORVM ·
QVI · SVNT · E · CONCILIO ·
HENRICVS · DVX · NORFOLCIAE ·
HENRICVS · MARCHIO · DE · LANSDOWNE ·
DOMINVS · IOANNES · RVSSELL ·
IOANNES · VICECOMES · DVDLEY · ET · WARD ·
GEORGIVS · BARO · DE · AVCKLAND ·
HONORABILIS · IAC · ABERCROMBIE ·
IACOBVS · MACKINTOSH · EQVES ·

ALEXANDER · BARING ·   GEORGIVS · BIRKBECK
HENRICVS · BROUGHAM ·   THOMAS · CAMPBELL
ISAAC · LYON · GOLDSMID · OLINTHUS · GREGORY
GEORGIVS · GROTE ·   IOSEPHVS · HUME ·
ZAC · MACAULAY ·   IACOBVS · MILL ·
BENIAMINVS · SHAW ·   IOHANNES · SMITH ·
GVLIELMVS · TOOKE ·   HENRICVS · WARBVRTON ·
HENRICVS · WAYMOUTH ·   IOANNES · WHISHAW ·
THOMAS · WILSON ·

GVLIELMVS · WILKINS · ARCHITECTVS ·

28. The inscription placed inside the foundation stone, the precise whereabouts of which are now unknown.

29. An invitation to the grand dinner in the Freemasons' Tavern following the foundation ceremony.

Plan of the Basement Ground Floor, & Upper Floor of the Centr

Ground Floor

North Court   South Court

Ground occupied by Workmen

North   Range

Inclosure for Workmen

South   Range

Upper Floor

Paved Footway   Carriage Road   Paved Footway
Iron Palisade   Iron Palisade

Gower Street North.

Grafton Street East.

E
N — S
W

1. } Ground Floor
2. } Porter's Lodge
3. } Lecture Rooms
4. }
5. Cloister
6. Professor's Room
7. Professor's Room
8. Professor's Room
9. Chemical Laboratory
10. Museum of Materia Medica

11. Theatre for Lectures.
12. } Lecture Rooms
13. }
14. Professor's Room
15. Professor's Room
16. Lower Vestibule
17. Cloister
18. } Lecture Rooms
19. }
20. University Office.

21. Clerks Room.
22. Council Room.
23. Museum of Botany &c.
24. Theatre for Lecture

25. } Basement
26. } Rooms for
27. } Anatomical School
28. }
29. Vault of Chemical Laboratory.

30. Vaults
31. } Students Common Ro
32. }
33. } Kitchens & room for
34. } Steward.
35. }
36. Vestibule
37. Refreshment Rooms
38. Stewards Room.

24

built

Ground occupied by Workmen.

25 26
28
27 29
30 *Vaults*

Basement
99 32 31
36 34
35 *Vaults*

Vaults 37

38
40 39

Upper Gower Street.

...usekeeper's Rooms.

Upper Floor
...heatre for Lectures
...ooms for Professor of
...natomy Surgery &c.
...useum of Anatomy
...useum of Natural History
...all.
...rofessor's Rooms.

49. *Vestibule.*
50. *Great Library.*
51. *Small Library.*
52. *Librarians Room.*
53. } *Rooms for*
54. } *Apparatus of*
55. } *Natural Philosophy*
56. *Professor's Room.*
57. *Theatre for Lectures.*
    North Court.
58. *Rooms for Anatomical School.*

30. The original plan for the College designed by William Wilkins.

31. The bust of William Wilkins by E. H. Bailey now in the Fitzwilliam Museum in Cambridge.

The architect chosen for the College was William Wilkins whose fashionable neo-Grecian design submitted in response to public advertisement in August 1825 was found exceedingly fine. Wilkins had previously designed new college buildings for Downing and King's at Cambridge, as well as Haileybury College. University College is Wilkins's greatest work, much more distinguished than the National Gallery he built in Trafalgar Square a few years later. The main entrance was to be at the top of a wide staircase under a ten-column Corinthian portico topped by an elegant dome. A chapel was conspicuous by its absence, the main entrance being intended to give on to the three principal rooms, the Museum of Natural History to the left, the Library to the right and the Great Hall directly ahead. Lecture theatres of various sizes led off generous cloisters running to the impressive wings containing further suites of rooms. In the event shortage of money meant that Wilkins's splendid design was only partially carried out.

The lowest tender received from a builder for the construction of Wilkins's building was £110,000, almost as much as the College had raised in toto by autumn 1826. 'The wish of the Council will appear to have been', it was confidently declared, 'rather to select a great design suited to the wants, the wealth, and the magnitude of the population for whom the Institution is intended, than one commensurate with its present means...' To this heroic decision the College owes the distinctive centre to its present rambling and otherwise unimpressive premises. It was decided to build the central range of the building with the portico and dome as envisaged by Wilkins, leaving over the addition of the two wings until the financial position improved. Together with the stone ornamentation, various fittings and the two front lodges the cost was not to exceed £86,000. Financial stringency also involved postponement of the Great Hall, and strict curtailment of expenditure on the Museum and Library, and thus the steps under the Portico became something of a lavish white elephant; 'the grandest entrance in London', it has been called, 'with nothing behind it'.

Despite the financial setbacks, the great hopes for the new institution continued. Before the building had begun, the College was treated to the publication of what he called its 'horoscope' by Thomas Babington Macaulay, the historian, in the pages of the *Edinburgh Review*. 'We predict', he wrote, 'that the clamour by which it has been assailed will die away, that it is destined to a long, a glorious, and a beneficent existence, that, while the spirit of its system remains unchanged, the details will vary with the varying necessities and facilities of every age, that it will be the model of many future establishments, that even those haughty foundations which now treat it with contempt, will in some degree feel its salutary influence, and that the approbation of a great people to whose wisdom, energy and virtue, its exertions will have largely contributed, will confer upon it a dignity more imposing than any which it would derive from the most lucrative patronage or the most splendid ceremonial.' A very rash prediction at the time, it turned out to be remarkably percipient.

35.

36. One of the engravings of the College buildings given a good deal of publicity in the late 1820s showing the wings with their supplementary domes as envisaged by Wilkins but never built for lack of funds.

37. Another such engraving by T. H. Shepherd, dedicated to the two founders of the College.

38. The College as it actually appeared at the time of its opening in 1828 and for nearly fifty years afterwards.

39. Another early engraving of the building showing the back – or east front – of the College, with the Cloisters before they were glazed in.

THE UNIVERSITY OF LONDON.

ho. H. Shepherd.

Engraved by

THE LONDON UNIVERSITY.

TO HENRY BROUGHAM ESQ. M.P. AND THOMAS CAMPBELL ESQ. TO WHOSE UNITED EXERTIONS,
LONDON IS INDEBTED FOR HER UNIVERSITY, THIS PLATE IS RESPECTFULLY INSCRIBED.

Published Nov. 15. 1828. by Jones & Cº Temple of the Muses. Finsbury Square, London.

38.

39.

EAST FRONT.

THE COCKNEY UNIVERSITY.
Tune—"Over the Water to Charley."

Come bustle, my neighbours, give over your labours,
    Leave digging and delving, and churning:
New lights are preparing to set you a staring,
    And fill all your noddles with learning.
Each Dustman shall speak, both in Latin and Greek,
    And Tinkers beat Bishops in knowledge—
If the opulent tribe will consent to subscribe
    To build up a new Cockney College.

We've had bubbles in milk—we've had bubbles in silk,
    And bubbles in baths of sea-water;
With other mad schemes, of rail-roads and steams,
    Of tombstones, and places for slaughter—
But none are so sure, so snug and secure,
    As this for which now we are burning,
For 'tis noble and wise to rub the world's eyes,
    And set all the Journeymen learning.

This notable scheme, as we've all of us seen,
    To enlighten the stall and the shamble,
Is twin to a dun-coloured dull Magazine,
    The offspring of Ritter Bann Campbell—
Has he wedded the Muse (I'm sure he'll excuse
    A truth which ought not to be hidden),
To publish such *Banns*, was the worst of all plans,
    Unless he had wished them forbidden.

This College, when formed, established, endowed,
    Will astonish each Radical's grannam,
Who may place her young fry in the midst of the crowd
    For two pounds ten shillings per annum.
And oh, what a thing, for a lad who climbs flues,
    Or for one who picks pockets of purses,
To woo in Ionic and Attic, the Muse,
    And make quires of bad Latin verses.

Hackney coachmen from *Swift* shall reply, if you feel
    Annoyed at being needlessly shaken;
And Butchers, of course, will be flippant from *Steele*,
    And Pig-drivers well versed in *Bacon*—
From *Locke* shall the Blacksmiths authority crave,
    And Gas-men cite *Coke* at discretion;
Undertakers talk *Gay* as they go to the *Grave*,
    And Watermen *Rowe*, by profession.

Burdett, who from *Oxford* received the degree
    Which in Scotland procured him such laurels,
Will lecture each Tuesday at half after three,
    On manners, and marriage, and morals;
Tom Creevy will teach the poor Sweeps how to dance,
    Lord Cochrane shall tutor the Sailors;
On horseback mad Law instruct Beggars to prance,
    And Fergusson manage the *Taylors!*

Pam Brougham shall teach mildness, and patience, and tact,
    And respect for the laws and his betters;
And Hume shall instruct them to add and subtract,
    While Wood teaches wisdom and letters.
On tactics of war civil Wilson shall speak,
    Lord Sefton shall ground them in driving,
And Mackintosh shew them three days in the week
    The easiest way to be thriving.

From a College like this, what advantage must spring,
    What strides will the people be taking;
Each cobbler will soon be as good as a King,
    And a King, a thing hardly worth making:
The rising of some, and the fall of the rest,
    Will bring things at last to their level;
And just as in France, which has suffered the test,
    Old England will go to the *Devil.*

THE COCKNEY COLLEGE.
AN INVITATION TO STINKOMALEE.
Tune—"*Run, Neighbours, run.*"

Run, sweepers, run, 'tis now the time for lecturing,
    Ev'ry man must learned be in these wise days;
Freedom's own island, shop-boys, recollect you're in,
    Whose native oaks we mean to graft with classic bays.
First of all discover (if you're able) where is Gower-street,
    The *terræ incognitæ* of Alfred-place and Store-street;
Get safely through Carmarthen-street, escape will be a mercy t'ye,
    And on your right, at number ten, you'll see the University.
        Run, sweepers, run, 'tis now the time for lecturing,
        Ev'ry man must learned be in these wise days.

'Tis there British genius, so admirably seconded,
    Soon shall blaze all o'er the world in glory bright,
Since Reason to Freedom so elegantly beckon did,
    To come and share the pleasures of dispensing light.
Conjointly there these Goddesses apprentice boys now call ye,
    Esquired by Messrs. Campbell, Grote, and Zachary Macaulay,
To study arts and sciences most fitted to your stations, sirs,
    And raise this isle of Britain to the wisest of all nations, sirs.
        Run, sweepers, run, 'tis now the time for lecturing,
        Ev'ry man must learned be in these wise days.

The tinkers soon shall worship Pan—while all the London shavers, Sirs,
    Disdain the unread *Barbari*, their *quondam* friends;
The cobblers, at Minerva's lap, turn *sutors* for her favours, Sirs,
    And leave un'tended, in their stalls, their soles and ends.
The milkmen publish scores of works on Blanco White and Paley,
    The tailors talk false quantities, and scribble fustian daily,
The pastry-cooks to *Tartarus* consign their ice and jellies, Sirs,
    And oyster-girls read *Milton's* works, or blasphemies, by *Shelly*, Sirs,
        Run, sweepers, run, 'tis now the time for lecturing,
        Ev'ry man must learned be in these wise days.

The postmen to *Belles Lettres* their attention then will turn all,
    And pot-boys study for the *bar* by which to live;
The ladder-mounting bricklayers by process *hodiernal*
    Enjoy the *Lime labor* which improvements give.
Butchers turned Aruspices, shall bow to link-boy Tages,
    And *accidence* be studied by the drivers of short stages;
Mantua-makers Virgil scan, in numbers most harmonious,
    And butchers boys set down their trays to work at *Suet-onius.*
        Run, sweepers, run, 'tis now the time for lecturing,
        Ev'ry man must learned be in these wise days.

To know his *Plato*, soon will be the butler's chief ambition, Sirs,
    In *Equity* our coachmen versed, to drive shall cease;
Fishmongers shall read from the *Delphin* large edition, Sirs,
    And poulterers on Turkey write, with plates of Greece.
Tallow-chandlers essays give on *dipthongs*, sure as fate, Sirs,
    And dustmen learn to venerate the ashes of the *great*, Sirs;
Pickle-men discuss Saint Paul, as easy as Salt Petre, Sirs,
    While coal-heavers shall count their sacks to every kind of metre, Sirs.
        Run, sweepers, run, 'tis now the time for lecturing,
        Ev'ry man must learned be in these wise days.

When those times arrive, quite different from now, my friends,
    Reason, worth, and learning, will assert their claims,
Duchesses will knead and wash, and Dukes will hold the plough, my friends,
    Fruitless will be titles then, and all high names;
Marquesses must clean their shoes, and Earls attend the stable, Sirs,
    Barons stir the kitchen fire, and Viscounts wait at table, sirs,
Come, then, boys—my shirtless boys, who love such gay diversity,
No Church, no King, no "*nothing else*," but Gow'r-street University.
        Run, sweepers, run, 'tis now the time for lecturing,
        Ev'ry man must learned be in these wise days.

Signed, on behalf of the Privy Council of Stinkomalee,
                    J. A.
                    H. B.
                    and
                    T. C.

COCKNEY COLLEGE

PⁱugΙn regarded the architecture of the College as pagan, adding acidly that it was 'in character with the intentions and principles of the institution'. The College had to put up with a good many snide remarks and attacks, especially in the crucial years between Campbell's letter in *The Times* in 1825 and the opening in 1828. The opposition was provoked partly by the apparent pretension of a joint-stock company masquerading as a university in a period of financial speculation; partly by the College's appeal to social groups excluded from the two old universities, an appeal intolerable to the Establishment; most of all, it was provoked by the rejection of all religious teaching and of compulsory religious conformity. The College soon became notorious in the words of Praed's poem as 'the radical infidel College', and more popularly and indelibly as 'the godless institution of Gower Street'.

40&41. Two of the verses ridiculing the idea of what was quickly dubbed 'the Cockney College' published in the ultra-Tory John Bull in July 1825 and January 1826, the latter by T. E. Hook. Some of the attacks on the College were mere guttersnipe outpourings of the Tory press, but these poems are relatively clever and amusing.

42. A cartoon lampooning the College published at the time of the foundation in February 1826. Brougham is shown hammering at the iron bar of philosophy on the anvil of public support, while Lord Lansdowne works the bellows and representatives of the populace are made to look on in what is clearly the wrong spirit.

UNIVERSITY OF LONDON.

41

The MEDICAL CLASSES *will open on* Wednesday *the 1st of October.*

ANATOMY AND OPERATIVE SURGERY—GRANVILLE S. PATTISON, Esq. Daily (except Saturday), from Two to Half-past Three. Fee, First Course £4; Second Course £3.

PHYSIOLOGY—CHARLES BELL, Esq. F.R.S. Three times a week, from Eleven to Twelve. Fee, First Course £3; Second Course £2.

NATURE AND TREATMENT OF DISEASES—JOHN CONOLLY, M.D. Daily (except Saturday), from Nine to Ten. Fee, First Course £3; Second Course £3.

MIDWIFERY AND DISEASES OF WOMEN AND CHILDREN—DAVID D. DAVIS, M.D. Four times a week, from Ten to Eleven. Fee, First Course £3; Second Course £3.

CLINICAL MEDICINE—THOMAS WATSON, M.D. Physician to the Middlesex Hospital. Twice a week, from Six to Seven P.M. Fee, £4.

SURGERY AND CLINICAL SURGERY—CHARLES BELL, Esq. Surgeon to the Middlesex Hospital. Three times a week, from Six to Seven P.M. Fee, £4.

MATERIA MEDICA AND PHARMACY—ANTHONY TODD THOMSON, M.D. Daily (except Saturday), from Eight to Nine A.M. Fee, First Course £3; Second Course £3.

CHEMISTRY—EDWARD TURNER, M.D. Daily, from Ten to Eleven, commencing on the 3rd of November. Fee, First Course £4; Second Course £3.

COMPARATIVE ANATOMY—ROBERT GRANT, M.D. Three times a week, from Three to Four. Fee, £5.

MEDICAL JURISPRUDENCE—JOHN GORDON SMITH, M.D. At the conclusion of the Winter and Spring Courses.

BOTANY—JOHN LINDLEY, Esq. F.R.S. At the conclusion of the Winter and Spring Courses. Fee, £4.

DISSECTIONS AND DEMONSTRATIONS—JAMES BENNETT, Esq. Daily. Fee, First Course £3; Second Course £2.

HOSPITAL PRACTICE—Middlesex Hospital, daily, from Half-past Twelve to Half-past One. Fee for the Academical Session £12 12s.

DISPENSARY PRACTICE—University Dispensary, daily, from Half-past Twelve to Half-past One. Fee for the Academical Session £5.

The Introductory Lectures of the Medical Professors will be delivered in the following order:

Three o'clock P.M. Wednesday, 1st of October—CHARLES BELL, Esq.
———— Thursday, 2nd of October—DR. CONOLLY.
———— Friday, 3rd of October—DR. DAVIS.
———— Saturday, 4th of October—GRANVILLE S. PATTISON, Esq.
———— Monday, 6th of October—DR. A. T. THOMSON.
———— Tuesday, 7th of October—DR. WATSON.

The Medical Classes will close in May, but each Professor will give a Winter and Spring Course.

When all the Introductory Lectures of the several Medical Classes shall have been delivered, the Professors will commence their Courses at the hours above stated.

The Certificates of the Medical Professors will be received at the College of Surgeons, and at Apothecaries' Hall. The Lectures will be open to students who may not desire certificates, or who wish merely to attend single Courses.

The names of Students are entered at the University Chambers, 29, Percy Street, Bedford Square. All other particulars respecting the Medical School may be obtained by application to the Professors, or to Mr. Coates at the Chambers.

(By Order of the Council.)

THOMAS COATES, *Clerk.*

N.B. The Fee for the First Courses will be required to be paid at whatever period of the Session the Pupil may enter.

Printed by RICHARD TAYLOR, Red Lion Court, Fleet Street.

43.

Though the building of the Portico and the Dome was not completed until the following year, the 'University of London' began its first academic session in October 1828. Selina Macaulay, daughter of Zachary, visited it in the middle of the first term and it impressed her as 'externally and internally a noble building'. She found 'the theatres extremely spacious and so arranged that it is much easier both to see and hear the lecturer than in any other building of the same size...' 'It seems so short a time', she concluded in her diary, 'since the whole scheme has been planned and executed that it reminds me of Aladdin's enchanted palace which sprung up in a single night...'

The opening inaugural lectures were well attended by the public and were pronounced a great success. The first of them was delivered on 1 October 1828 by Charles Bell, the Professor of Surgery and the most famous member of the distinguished Medical Faculty that had been assembled. He had been educated at Edinburgh, becoming a member of the Speculative Society there, that notable group brought together in the 1790s which was to provide the London University with no less than five members of the original Council and three of the first professors. He conducted important research on the working of the nervous system and became a surgeon of repute at the Middlesex Hospital. John Conolly too studied medicine at Edinburgh, graduating in 1821 and subsequently practising medicine at Stratford-on-Avon, twice becoming mayor of the town. Neither Bell nor Conolly were to stay long at the College owing to the unfortunate quarrels which soon engulfed the Medical Faculty. Bell resigned in 1830, going to build up the medical school at the Middlesex and then returning to Edinburgh University. Conolly resigned in 1831, later taking charge of the Hanwell Lunatic Asylum where he introduced humane methods of treatment for the insane and pioneered revolutionary changes in this field. His pupil and son-in-law Henry Maudsley (who qualified at UCL in 1856 and became Professor of Medical Jurisprudence, 1869-80) was to be commemorated by the Maudsley Hospital.

44. Sir Charles Bell, FRS, the Professor of Physiology and Surgery, who gave the first inaugural lecture in October 1828.

45. John Conolly, the Professor of the Nature and Treatment of Disease, who gave the second of the inaugural lectures.

44.

45.

46.

47.

48.

46. Anthony Todd Thomson, Professor of Materia Medica from the opening of the College until his death in 1849.

47. Robert E. Grant, FRS, Professor of Comparative Anatomy (to which Zoology was later added) from the opening of the College until his death in 1874.

48. David D. Davis, Professor of Midwifery from the opening of the College until his death in 1841, as portrayed in the bust in the library of the Medical School.

A contemporary of Bell's at Edinburgh, Anthony Todd Thomson, became Professor of Materia Medica. He too had come to London in the first decade of the nineteenth century to make his mark in the medical profession, and also in the literary world. He conducted original research into the composition of alkaloids and iodides, and published a good deal. David D. Davis, a Glasgow graduate of Welsh origin, became Professor of Midwifery and Diseases of Women and Children. He had established himself as a successful London obstetrician, becoming a leading private teacher of the subject and pioneering many advanced methods, especially associated with obstetric forceps. He achieved some prominence by delivering the future Queen Victoria at Kensington Palace in 1819.

Robert E. Grant was appointed Professor of Comparative Anatomy at the time of the opening and he remained in this post until his death forty-six years later in 1874 as the longest survivor of the original professoriate. Throughout this period he gave five lectures a week and was believed never to have missed one. Imposing if eccentric in appearance, he invariably wore full evening dress. He was yet another Edinburgh graduate and had done important research there prior to coming to the College, especially on sponges, a genus of which is named after him. In London he gave his students breakfast in his house near Euston and took favoured ones on continental walking-tours, but he did little further research. A friend of Darwin and Cuvier, he remained on the fringes of the forefront of his subject. He left his valuable collection of early books on biology to the College.

THE EDITOR OF "THE CABINET CYCLOPEDIA".

49. The encyclopaedic Revd
Dionysius Lardner, FRS, Professor
of Natural Philosophy and
Astronomy, 1828-31, as pictured in
Fraser's Magazine after his
resignation.

50. A registration card for
Lardner's class in the first session.

The first holder of the Chair of Natural Philosophy was the Revd Dr Dionysius Lardner, an extraordinary man who has been described as making up in contemporary notoriety what he lacked in more lasting fame. He moved in the most fashionable literary and political circles, and was very successful as a popular lecturer and writer of great zest. His best-known work is the *Cabinet Cyclopaedia* which he edited in 133 volumes between 1829 and 1849. His early lectures at the College attracted a good deal of attention, but Lardner, his apparatus, his courses and his salary caused more trouble for the Council than any other topic in the opening years. He resigned in 1831 to make more money from writing and giving lectures in the USA. He subsequently eloped with the wife of a cavalry officer, becoming involved in very expensive law-suits and having to settle in Paris.

He cut rather more dash in life than many of his academic successors.

Only 21 and just down from Cambridge, Augustus De Morgan was the youngest of the original professors when he was appointed to the Chair of Mathematics. He was to distinguish himself by resigning from this position on a matter of principle not once, but twice. For many, however, he was the outstanding figure in the first generation of the life of the College. Sir Henry Roscoe, the chemist who was a student at the College in the 1840s, called him 'one of the profoundest and subtlest thinkers of the nineteenth century'.

De Morgan taught logic and mathematics with a deft brilliance and penetration that his students found inescapably fascinating, and he exerted a captivating influence on many of them, including W. S. Jevons and Walter Bagehot. A prolific writer, who made a key contribution to the development of modern symbolic logic, he was also a leading member of the Astronomical Society and the first President of the London Mathematical Society. He was a great wit too.

When Sir George Cornewall Lewis as Chancellor of the Exchequer in the 1850s rejected a proposal for the decimalisation of the coinage on the grounds of the complexity of various schemes, De Morgan scornfully drew up a variety of proposals in which ten farthings would make a what's-its-name, ten what's-its-names a how-d'ye-call-it and ten howd'ye-call-its a thingeme-bob, or ten farthings a George, ten Georges a Cornewall and ten Cornewalls a Lewis.

De Morgan resigned in 1831 over the unhappy Pattison affair (see p. 43). After the early death of his successor in 1836, he returned to the Chair and held it for thirty years until his second resignation in 1867. The Council's rejection of the appointment of James Martineau as Professor of Mental Philosophy and Logic on the grounds that he was a Unitarian minister was, he argued, itself an ironical but fundamental desertion of the principles on which the College had been founded. He felt this so strongly that he refused to allow a bust or portrait of himself to be placed in the College to which he had brought such distinction.

D istinguished appointments were also made in chemistry and in botany. Yet a further Edinburgh medical graduate, Edward Turner, was appointed as the first Professor of Chemistry. He was rapidly to attain a European reputation in this subject. During his tenure of the Chair he was occupied in analytical work on the determination of atomic weights and in the writing of two textbooks, one of which, *The Elements of Chemistry*, came to be the standard work for many years. It was translated into German, and later edited by the great German chemist Liebig. Turner was also active in the Geological Society and began the teaching of geology in the College. He died at the early age of 39 in 1837.

John Lindley was the first Professor of Botany, a subject originally conceived as an adjunct to the teaching of medicine. Lindley was the son of a Norfolk horticulturalist and was not himself a graduate. Employed originally by a seed merchant, he became librarian to Sir Joseph Banks, the noted naturalist and President of the Royal Society from 1822. His greatest contribution to the subject derived from the success of his efforts to preserve the Royal Botanic Gardens in Kew in the late 1830s. His *Vegetable Kingdom* and *Introduction to Botany* enjoyed a long period as standard works. The contrast was noted between his own appearance, fresh, ruddy and hale-looking, and that of the students.

53.

52.

52. *Edward Turner, FRS, Professor of Chemistry, 1828-37, whose bust by Butler remains in the Chemistry Department.*

53. *John Lindley, FRS, Professor of Botany, 1828-60.*

54.

55.

The most striking characteristic of the twenty-four professors who constituted the teaching body of the College when it opened in 1828 was their relative youth. All but three were aged under 40, and six were 30 or under. The second striking fact is the number of posts in subjects which had not previously been taught in English universities, or, more significantly still, in British universities, and even European ones. The chairs in the modern foreign languages and in English language and literature were all especially notable innovations.

P. F. Merlet, the original teacher of French, was not given the title of professor until 1834, but chairs in German, Italian, Spanish and English, as well as in Latin, Greek, Hebrew and Hindustani, were established from the outset. The modern languages were taught by refugees from their respective countries. German was taught by Ludwig von Mühlenfels, a progressive and independent thinker, who was appointed while passing through London on his way to join a band of fellow exiles in Mexico, having escaped from a Prussian political prison.

54. The first of four of the original professors in what was to become the Faculty of Arts, all portrayed at much later stages in their unusual careers, after they had left the College: Sir Antonio Panizzi, Professor of Italian, 1828-38.

55. Antonio Alcalá Galiano, Professor of Spanish, 1828-30.

56. The Revd Thomas Dale, Professor of English, 1828-30.

57. George Long, Professor of Greek, 1828-31, and later Professor of Latin, 1842-46.

Italian was put in the hands of Antonio Panizzi, who had escaped from a death sentence in Italy. Besides his post in the College, Panizzi took that of Assistant Librarian at the British Museum in 1831, becoming Keeper of Printed Books there in 1837 and eventually Principal Librarian in 1856. After giving up his Chair, he achieved permanent fame as virtual creator of both the library catalogue and the Reading Room at the British Museum. Spanish was handled by Antonio Alcalá Galiano, a marked man in Spain after 1832 when he moved a resolution against Ferdinand VII in the Spanish parliament and as a result was sentenced to death. A leading figure in Spanish Romantic literature, Alcalá resigned in 1830 to go to Paris hoping to take part in the July Revolution. In 1831 von Mühlenfels also left hoping for an improved political climate in Germany. His successors in the Chair of German were of little or no consequence for many years, while Spanish was not taught again after 1830 until the establishment of the present Department in 1964.

Thomas Dale, the first Professor of English, took his holy orders very seriously and evangelically. 'I shall invariably aim', he announced in his inaugural lecture, 'to impart moral as well as intellectual instruction... I shall esteem it my duty... to inculcate lessons of virtue'. After two years of grappling with this task, he departed to devote himself to the ministry, becoming vicar of St Bride's, Fleet Street, and later of St Pancras. Between 1836 and 1839 he was also to find what was doubtless a more receptive audience for his inculcation of lessons of virtue as the first Professor of English at King's College, London.

George Long, the original Professor of Greek, was a more significant figure. He had been recruited from Trinity College, Cambridge, to be the founding Professor of Ancient Languages at the University of Virginia. He returned to England to take the Chair of Greek, but then resigned over the Pattison affair in 1831 and worked full-time for the Society for the Diffusion of Useful Knowledge as editor of the *Quarterly Journal of Education* and then of the famous twenty-nine-volume *Penny Cyclopaedia*. He was to return to UCL as Professor of Latin for four years in the 1840s, but left again to combine school-teaching in Brighton with his literary and scholarly work.

56.

57.

The study of the workings of society was naturally not to be ignored in a College so influenced by utilitarian thought. In law and in economics distinguished appointments were made at the outset. Law was taken to be an important subject of study from the very beginning, and the College can fairly claim to have inaugurated the systematic university study of law. To the Chair of Jurisprudence John Austin was appointed in July 1827, and he then spent a year in Bonn preparing his lectures while mixing with the great German scholars and jurists there. Austin was recognised as a powerful intellect, and his deep learning and original thought duly impressed the students (including John Stuart Mill). But he completed very little in his lifetime, not even managing the preparation of his lectures for publication, a task his wife had to finish after his death in 1859. After the demand for the law classes had apparently fallen away, Austin left the College, becoming first a member of the Criminal Law Commission, later conducting an inquiry into the state of Malta, subsequently living in Germany and France. The other law professor, Andrew Amos, also held very popular and well-attended classes for the first sessions, but also left after enrolment collapsed. A successful barrister, he had earlier been Shelley's only friend at Eton and was later a county court judge and

58.

58. The bust of Andrew Amos, Professor of English Law, 1828-34, presented by his former students and still kept in the Laws Faculty.

59. The certificate of appointment of John Austin as Professor of Jurisprudence, a post he was to hold until 1835.

59.

University of London.

THE COUNCIL THIS DAY APPOINTED

John Austin Esquire

Barrister at Law

Professor

OF

Jurisprudence

By order of the Council

London, the 12th day of July 1827

Warden.

Chairman.

a professor at Cambridge. His son, Sheldon Amos, was Professor of Jurisprudence at the College, 1869-78, and his grandson, Sir Maurice Sheldon Amos, was Quain Professor of Comparative Law, 1932-37.

In economics the same story is repeated of high hopes unrealised despite an outstanding appointment. J. R. McCulloch was the first professional economist in the sense of one who made his living from the subject as journalist, author and teacher. An Edinburgh man, he was appointed to the Chair of Political Economy after coming to London to give the lectures established as an independent memorial to David Ricardo. McCulloch soon embarked on a prolonged dispute with the Council about his salary, eventually refusing to lecture after 1835 unless it were guaranteed at a higher level than the fees from the small number of students who attended. In 1837 his Chair was declared vacant.

Notable among the original appointments was that of F. A. Rosen, who brought the best of German scholarship to the College introducing notions basic to comparative philology. Professor of Oriental Literature at 22, he was later Professor of Sanskrit for the two years before his early death in 1837. Teaching of various Oriental languages continued until 1917 when they were transferred to the new institution that became the School of Oriental and African Studies.

60.

61.

60. J. R. McCulloch, Professor of Political Economy, 1828-37, painted clasping respectfully a copy of Adam Smith's Wealth of Nations.

61. The elegant bust of Friedrich August Rosen, Professor of Oriental Literature until 1831 and then of Sanskrit, 1835-37; he also worked for the British Museum where this bust remains today.

The three years of hopeful expectation prior to the opening gave way after 1828 to three years fraught with many problems and wasteful quarrels. The only sources of finance were, first, what could be raised through shares or donations as capital and secondly, what the fees of the students brought in as income. The capital was splendidly but unwisely used up by the cost of the site and the building. 'The expenditure has been lavish', wrote John Austin's wife in 1830, 'the plans are ill-digested, and vibrating, like all things in which the Whigs have a hand, between the desire of being popular and the fear of being unfashionable...' Professorial dependence on a proportion of the fees meant, when fewer students than expected enrolled, that their incomes were unacceptably low, and the Council's guarantees of at least £300 a year were hard to meet. The grievances of the teachers were compounded by their not having any formal status as a body or any say in the running of the College, and by the

attitude of the Warden.

The first appointment made by the Council had been that of Leonard Horner as Warden in May 1827. Horner came, like so many of the others, from Edinburgh, where he was regarded as 'one of the most useful citizens that Edinburgh ever possessed'. He was the founder of the School of Arts there in 1821, now Heriot-Watt University, and was an energetic Secretary of the Geological Society in London from 1810. From the start, however, he took a high-handed view of his new office. The generous salary of £1,200 a year on which he had insisted was itself a source of irritation to the professors, and Horner's continual petty interference in their work proved increasingly objectionable.

Matters came to a head in 1830-31 over the complicated issues raised by the criticisms against Granville Sharp Pattison, the Professor of Anatomy. The medical students were provoked by what they saw as Pattison's incompetence both as an

Wednesday. Oct. 27. 1830.

Sir,

Understanding that D? Thomson, Senior, is giving out that I am insane, I think it appropriate to inform you that he said the same thing of you, at a meeting of the Professors, last year.

Your obedient servant

J. Gordon Smith.

L? Horner Esq?

63.

62. The most idyllic of the early prints of the College, again showing the wings as Wilkins planned them, but as they never were.

63. Evidence that life in the College was no idyll: a letter addressed to the Warden at the start of the third session by J. Gordon Smith, Professor of Medical Jurisprudence, 1829-32, one of the first of the professors to become an alcoholic and perhaps the only one to die in a debtor's prison.

64. The focus of many of the early quarrels: Leonard Horner, FRS, (1785-1864), the first and only Warden, 1827-31.

64.

anatomist and as a teacher (when he did turn up to lecture, he did so in hunting pink) and their opinions were supported by Charles Bell. Horner's clumsy attempts to sack Pattison, however, led to the case being taken up by the other aggrieved professors as a stick to beat Horner with.

The issue gathered, as such disputes do, many bitter subtleties. It led to the first student demonstration, in 1830, and eventually caused the resignations not only of Bell and Conolly from the Medical Faculty, but, following the dismissal of Pattison, of De Morgan, Long and Rosen too. In the end Horner himself was forced to resign and the office of Warden was abolished, being replaced by a Secretary at £200. Horner had a distinguished career later as the first Factory Inspector. The Pattison affair had many consequences; one of them was that the professors were organised into a Senate and into Faculties; another was that the College was to manage without a full-time head for the rest of the century.

KINGS COLLEGE VERSUS LONDON UNIVERSITY
or Which is the Weightiest

Lying behind the financial difficulties of the early years was the problem of student numbers. There had been talk of providing for 2,000 students; at least 1,100 were deemed necessary in order to balance the books in the first year: in fact, 641 materialised in 1828-29 (this total for the first year has recently been re-calculated; it was previously thought to be only 624), and only about 630 in the following year. Thereafter they fluctuated rather, and did not begin to increase substantially until the 1870s. It took over eighty years to reach the projected 2,000 (see the graph on p.231).

If imitation implies success, however, the College achieved it before the doors were opened. An Establishment rival in the form of King's College began at a meeting in June 1828 chaired by the Duke of Wellington and attended by no less than three archbishops, seven bishops and 'the principal nobility'. The prime founder was the Revd Dr George D'Oyly, the Rector of Lambeth, who had been much disturbed by the exclusion of religious teaching from the curriculum of a University of London. D'Oyly believed that the Church of England 'presents Christianity in its most pure and perfect form', and that the interests of the Church and the State combined to demand a new institution with different principles to those adopted in Gower Street. With the backing he naturally received, there was no difficulty about obtaining a charter in 1829. A new wing was built to Somerset House in the Strand and by October 1831 a second institution of higher education was opened in London. A healthy rivalry has been maintained between the two colleges ever since.

65. A cartoon portraying the initial antagonism between the College and the rival King's College founded in 1828: a clutch of bloated bishops, including the Archbishop of Canterbury and the Revd Dr George D'Oyly, with the added weight of Money and Interest, are pitted against the founders of University College, including Brougham (waving the broom) and Bentham (clad in dressing gown), supported by Sense and Science.

66.

Date of Entry.	No.	Name of Student.	Age.	Native of.	Address in London.	Nominated by.	Classes.
1828 June 12	1	Charles Z. Macaulay	15	London	50. Great Ormond Street	Zachary Macaulay Esqr	Junior Latin, Greek, Arithm's English Matric't
June 12	2	James B. Mill	14	London	1 Queen Square West	James Mill Esqr	Junior Latin, Greek, Arithm's Matric't
June 12	3	Frederick D. Goldsmid	16	London	Dulwich Hill House Camberwell	I. L. Goldsmid Esqr	Junior Latin, Greek, Arith, Senior Hebrew
June 16	4	Goxham Smith	16	London	Stoke Newington	Rich'd Smith Esqr	Junior Latin, Greek, Maths, French Matriculation

66. The first entries in the register of students for the opening session in 1828: they represent the youthful offspring of some illustrious names in the history of the College.

67.

The system of education established at the College was based upon instruction by means of lectures and upon written examinations. This was a deliberate departure from the method of the older English universities; it was modelled on the practice of Scotland and of Germany. The early years saw an enormous amount of lecturing taking place. The naturalist and Registrar of the University, W. B. Carpenter, as a student in the early 1830s attended no less than thirty-five lectures a week. There was some bleak justification for Coleridge's contemptuous reference to the College as a 'lecture-bazaar'.

Initially no degrees were offered. There was in 1830 a proposal to award the cumbersome degree of *M.Med. et Chir. U.L.*, but the absence of a royal charter was generally held to deny degree-giving powers to a body that had no outside authority for calling itself a university. Instead Certificates of Honours were presented in connection with each course, and a General Certificate was obtainable after three years of following an agreed programme of study. Fees were payable for each separate course of lectures. The average cost for a student nominated by a proprietor (such students were admitted at a lower rate) was approximately £22 7s. 6d. per annum, an amount it would have taken, say, a coachman a year to earn. The College was thus well beyond the means of the working class.

67. A late nineteenth-century photograph of the Botanical Theatre, one of the four main lecture theatres in the semi-circular projections at the rear of the College, showing it a little more drab perhaps, but not substantially different from its original appearance.

68. A Certificate of Honours as awarded in the early years.

69. The elaborate regulations for what seem to have been the first examinations, held at Christmas 1829.

68.

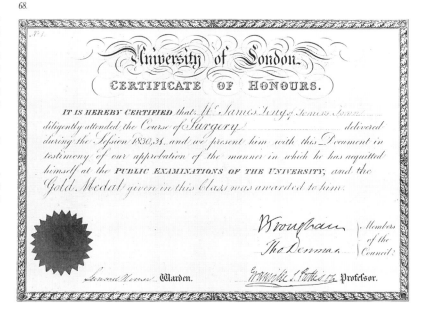

46

UNIVERSITY OF LONDON.

EXAMINATIONS,

Which must be attended by every Student who is desirous of obtaining a Prize or Certificate of Honour at the Close of the Session.

IN all Examinations in which the Questions are to be answered in writing, the Answers must be signed with a private mark. Instead of a Motto, as used last year, it is proposed to substitute a Number, as being more convenient. A series of Numbers will belong to each Class. The Numbers will be put up in sealed packets, and each Student will take one from a box in presence of the Professor. He will thus have a separate Number for each Class he attends.

The Student must be careful not to communicate his Numbers to any one. As soon as he has obtained them, he must write his *name, designation,* and *address in London,* upon a sheet of letter-paper, fold it in the form of a letter, seal it with wax, and mark the outside thus :

" To The Warden—*Latin*"
No. 5

according to the Number he has drawn. There must be a separate packet for each Class. Thus the Student may send in two or more packets, and they must all be inscribed in a similar manner, thus :

" To The Warden—*Latin*"   " To The Warden—*Greek*"
No. 5   No. 20

These packets must be left at the Office immediately after the Numbers have been drawn.

The written Answers to the Questions given out in each Class must be signed with the Number which the Student has drawn for that Class.

The packets will be opened at the Public Meeting, when the Numbers to which the Prizes have been awarded shall be declared.

[*turn over.*

CHRISTMAS EXAMINATIONS. 1829.

Classes of LATIN, GREEK, ENGLISH, FRENCH, GERMAN, MATHEMATICS, NATURAL PHILOSOPHY, ENGLISH LAW. The Examinations of the Junior and Senior Classes will take place at the same time.

Latin.—Tuesday, Dec. 22, at Half past Nine o'Clock, A.M.
Greek.—Wednesday, Dec. 23, at Two o'Clock.
English.—Saturday, Dec. 19, at Ten o'Clock, A.M.
French.—Monday, Dec. 21, at Two o'Clock.
German.—Tuesday, Dec. 22, at Half past Eight o'Clock, A.M.
Mathematics.—Wednesday, Dec. 23, at Half past Nine o'Clock, A.M.
Natural Philosophy.—Saturday, Dec. 19, at Two o'Clock.
English Law.—Tuesday the 5th and Wednesday the 6th of January, at Six o'Clock in the evening.

In all the above Classes the Answers to the Questions at this Examination will be taken into consideration in the determination of the Prizes at the close of the Session.

MEDICAL CLASSES.

The Examinations will take place in the Second Week of January. The days and hours will be announced hereafter.

N. B. *No Student who obtained a Gold Medal or First Prize last Session can be allowed to contend for a Prize in the same Class in the present Session. And no Student who obtained a Silver Medal or Second Prize last Session shall be entitled to receive a similar Prize in the same Class in the present Session.*

(By Order of the Council.)

LEONARD HORNER, *Warden.*

University of London,
8th Dec. 1829.

A series of Questions for the Students of each Professor will be printed, of which a Copy will be delivered to the Student after he is in the Examination-Room.

The Answers must be written in the Examination-Room, and they will be collected at one time. No Book must be brought into the room.

The Student must bring pen and ink. The Answers must be written in books of uniform size, which are to be had at Mr. Taylor's, Bookseller, 30 Upper Gower Street.

Printed by RICHARD TAYLOR, Red Lion Court, Fleet Street.

70.

70. Both sides of a gold medal as awarded to the best student in every subject.

71. The playground of University College School as it appeared in an engraving by the German-born artist George Scharf published in 1833. Scharf's son – later Sir George Scharf, the first director of the National Portrait Gallery – was a pupil at the School.

A school was established in connection with the College in 1830, and from the start it prospered at a time when the College was not otherwise growing. Opened in a Gower Street house with eighty boys in the first term, a year later the School had 249 boys and accommodation had to be found within the main building. After 1832 in an unforeseen way the School came to take up a good deal of space in the College, particularly in the area originally intended for the Great Hall and the rooms below it. Thomas Hewitt Key and Henry Malden, Professors of Latin and Greek, were put in joint charge of the School once its success was evident.

Key, very versatile in his interests, had been the first Professor of Mathematics at

71.

72.

73.

the University of Virginia, and in 1842 gave up the Chair of Latin at UCL for that of Comparative Grammar – the first such chair in England, though his scholarship in this field was not beyond question; he combined this post with that of Headmaster until the day of his death in 1875. He was a great and vigorous teacher, while Malden was the more careful and urbane scholar. Malden gave up the joint headship in 1842, though he continued to teach the Sixth until 1868.

Other professors also taught at the School, which quickly built up a considerable reputation for religious tolerance, a broad curriculum and a sympathetic relationship between teacher and pupil. It was one of the earliest schools to attempt to dissociate education and flogging.

UNIVERSITY OF LONDON.

Page

REGULATIONS FOR THE LIBRARY.

◆

I. *Perfect silence must be maintained.*

II. If any Gentleman wishes for a Book, he must write the title on a slip of paper, and give it to the Assistant in attendance, for the Librarian.

III. When a Gentleman has finished reading a Book, he must return it to the Assistant in attendance.

IV. If Gentlemen wish to make Extracts, they must not place their paper *on* a Book in writing the extract.

V. The Library is accessible from *Ten* in the Morning until *Four* in the Afternoon.

(By Order of the Council.)

F. A. COX,

LIBRARIAN.

74

The first Librarian of the College was the Revd Dr F. A. Cox, the original Secretary of the Council. By the beginning of 1829 he had judiciously built up a collection of some 6,500 volumes. A year later there were 9,027 volumes. 'The Council would gladly have announced a larger addition', recorded the *Annual Report* for 1830, 'but prudential considerations have limited the purchases.' The books were housed in what was called the Small Library at the southern end of the building, since funds were inadequate for the proposed Great Library. A further economy in 1831 was to dispense with the services of the Librarian: there was to be no proper successor until 1871, the Library being left in the charge of an assistant and sometimes simply of a beadle. Less than £50 altogether was spent on books in the poverty-stricken four years 1832-35, and the average annual expenditure for the forty-three years from 1832 to 1875 was a mere £51.

In this period, growth was therefore heavily dependent on donations and bequests. Some 4,000 books came from Jeremy Bentham in 1833, and Joseph Hume's large collection of tracts followed in 1855. An impressive number of collections were left by professors of the College, the earliest really notable one being that left by

74. The earliest Library Regulations issued soon after the opening of the Library in January 1829.

75. Capt Alexander Maconochie, RN, the first Professor of Geography, 1833-36.

76. J. T. Graves, FRS, Professor of Jurisprudence, 1839-43.

J. T. Graves in 1870. Despite being Professor of Jurisprudence and later a Poor Law Inspector, Graves formed a valuable library of over 14,000 items chiefly devoted to early mathematics. His sister married Leopold von Ranke, the founder of modern historical method, and he was a forebear of Robert Graves. He once compiled a list of 2,862 anagrams on the name of Augustus De Morgan in English, Latin, French and German.

The 1830s saw retrenchment on other fronts besides that of the Library. No initial appointment had been made in history, and the Chair was not filled until 1830, and then only briefly and inadequately by a retired headmaster. There was no regular history teaching until after 1834. One of the few developments of the period, other than the School and the Hospital, was in geography, though as it turned out even this was abortive. In 1833 Alexander Maconochie, Secretary of the newly-founded Royal Geographical Society, was made the first Professor of Geography in the College – and the first in Britain. A retired naval captain, he left in 1836 to go to administer Van Diemen's Land and to investigate penal conditions. No successor was appointed, and geography was not revived at the College until 1903.

77. A hospital had been regarded by the Medical Faculty from the beginning as an essential part of the College, but for some years they had to put up with the limited facilities offered by the University Dispensary in Upper Gower Street. Plans for the building of the 'North London Hospital' on the unused part of the College site on the other side of Gower Street were accepted in 1832, and the foundation stone was laid in May 1833 by the Duke of Somerset, FRS, President of the Royal Institution and the then Chairman of the Council of the College. George Scharf was present and recorded the occasion in a sketch.

77.

78.

W illiam Sharpey's active tenure of his Chair for nearly forty years earned for him the title of the father of modern physiology in Britain. Before being appointed in 1836, he had been trained at Edinburgh and had studied at the French and German universities where physiology was much more highly developed than it was in Britain before his own lifetime. He was a thorough and inspiring teacher. He hardly ever showed an experiment or piece of apparatus in classes, but he was one of the first to introduce the microscope for practical illustration of his teaching, having a table especially constructed for this purpose. He exerted a considerable influence through his students, who came to dominate the subject (see p. 86), and through being for twenty years after 1853 a powerful and effective Secretary of the Royal Society.

Sharpey's Chair was nominally in anatomy as well as physiology, but anatomy was primarily in other hands. After Charles Bell's resignation it was taught by two brothers – Jones Quain, Sharpey's predecessor as Professor of Anatomy and Physiology, and Richard Quain, Demonstrator, 1831-2, then Professor of Anatomy, 1831-50, and later surgeon at the Hospital, Professor of Clinical Surgery, 1850-66, and President of the Royal College of Surgeons. He is remembered as founder of the Quain chairs and for presenting the law library of his half-brother, Sir John Richard Quain, a judge and himself a former student of the College. Many of Bell's preserved anatomical and pathological specimens were

79.

78. William Sharpey, FRS, Professor of Anatomy and Physiology, 1836-74 – 'an enlarged edition of Mr Pickwick' – photographed soon after his retirement.

79. Sharpey's specially constructed table – preserved in the Department of Physiology – which enabled a microscope to be passed round a number of students.

80. A drawing by George Scharf of the Hospital soon after its completion, showing the gate maintained across the part of Gower Street owned by the College. The roadway was eventually sold in 1892 to St Pancras for the large sum of £15,000.

81. John Elliotson, FRS, the advanced but controversial Professor of Medicine, 1831-39.

acquired by the College before his resignation as the beginnings of the Anatomy Museum (see p. 87); some are still in use at the Medical School.

The first stage of the Hospital was opened in November 1834 with beds for 130 patients. It was built for less than £7,600, much more cheaply than the College itself: 'all architectural decorations', it was plainly stated, 'have for the sake of economy been studiously excluded'. The building was financed entirely through public appeals at a time when the College was seriously in debt. The intimate connection with the College was recognised in 1837 when its name was changed to 'University College Hospital'. A southern extension was added in 1841 and a northern one in 1846.

Much of the early success of the new Hospital was due to John Elliotson, Conolly's successor in 1831 with the title of Professor of the Theory and Practice of Medicine. Elliotson was exceedingly popular as a teacher and was a practitioner of great energy and originality. He was a pioneer of the stethoscope and he introduced the used of quinine for malaria. With the best of scientific intentions, however, he got involved in the earliest of the scandals arising from the Victorian mesmerism craze. The two Okey sisters threw hystero-epileptic fits and were put into mesmeric

trances before large and fashionable audiences, attracting much attention, including that of Charles Dickens. The College found it all rather embarrassing, even before the *Lancet* exposed the sisters as fakes. Elliotson had to make an untimely resignation.

82. A watercolour picture of the
College from Old Gower Mews (the
site of Foster Court) painted by
George Sidney Shepherd in 1835.
Behind the dome can be seen the
uncompleted Great Hall, later
destroyed by fire. The picture was
bought by the College in 1988.

84.

83. The examination in July 1842 for matriculation in the new degree-giving University of London.

84. The Royal Charter granted to the College in 1836.

O n 28 November 1836 a Royal Charter was at length granted by the Whig government which included, in Lord Lansdowne and Lord John Russell, two of the members of the College's founding Council. The opposition of Oxford and Cambridge to the award of degrees to non-members of the established Church was overcome; so too was that of the various hospital medical schools in London to the exclusive power of awarding medical degrees. These problems, and that of the existence of King's College, were solved by establishing an entirely new body as the 'University of London'. The College gave up this, its original title, taking that of University College, a style first suggested in the medical press in 1833, though a possibly misleading one in that it suggests an Oxbridge rather than a continental or a Scottish model. Later the same day, another Charter was granted to the new University of London empowering it to award degrees in Arts, Laws and Medicine to students of both UCL and King's, besides such other institutions as might be approved later on. It was a sensible compromise, but the separation of teaching and examining stored up great difficulties for the future.

Engineering was one of the first victims of the College's financial insecurity. John Millington had been announced as professor of the subject in 1827, but he resigned before the opening when the Council refused to guarantee him an adequate income. Not until 1841 was a chair of Civil Engineering established, the first of its kind in the country. The period of intensive railway building had started, and the first professor, C. B. Vignoles, was a leading railway engineer and inventor of the 'Vignoles rail'. He came to UCL having lost £80,000 in shares while Chief Engineer on the Sheffield and Manchester Railway. He was later responsible for the construction of railways in many part of the world, especially in Russia, where he built the Dnieper suspension bridge at Kiev, the largest of its kind in the world.

Two distinguished figures in other fields of engineering were appointed to new chairs in 1847. Both came from near Manchester, where they had sat at the feet of John Dalton and the inquiring scientific community there; neither was a successful teacher. Eaton Hodgkinson, who had started out as a pawnbroker in Salford, became the first Professor of Mechanical Engineering. He invented an important new type of cast-iron girder, the forerunner of the modern I-beam, and worked with Stephenson on the Menai bridge.

Bennet Woodcroft worked originally in his family textile firm, but made a range of ingenious inventions and became a consulting engineer. His great work was the creation of the modern Patent Office, to which he devoted himself after resigning the Chair of Machinery in 1851. The valuable collection of mechanical models which the Society of Arts had given for him to form a Machinery Museum in the College found their way, without apparent authority, to the Patent Office Museum and later to the Science Museum.

85. Bennet Woodcroft, FRS, who between 1847 and 1851 enjoyed the distinctive title of Professor of Machinery.

86. Charles Blacker Vignoles, FRS, the first Professor of Civil Engineering, 1841-45.

In 1846, Lord Brougham was obliged to say that his anticipations of success for the College twenty years previously had not been realised. Yet while the impoverished 1830s had seen major developments in the School and the Hospital, the barely better endowed 1840s saw the first new buildings for the College itself in the shape of the new General Library and the new Chemistry Laboratory. The latter, the first purpose-built teaching laboratory for chemistry in the country, was a particularly important innovation.

Turner's successor as Professor of Chemistry in 1836 was Thomas Graham, a chemist of real distinction. 'If along the great highroad of Chemistry', one of his own successors stated later, 'temples were erected to the memory of the master minds who moulded and guided the science forward into the unknown future, one of the greatest of these would be to the memory of

87. The Birkbeck Laboratory, the College's first teaching laboratory for chemistry, as pictured in the Illustrated London News *soon after its opening in 1846. It was subsequently used by the Department of Botany and latterly Physics until its demolition in 1968.*

87.

Thomas Graham'. Educated at both Glasgow and Edinburgh, he worked on the fundamental problems of the ultimate particles of matter and the diffusion of gases, formulating the earliest modern understanding of these questions. He was one of the founders and first President of the Chemical Society in 1841. He also started the teaching of chemistry through the practical system of personal experiment by the student. Liebig's pioneering laboratory at Giessen was earlier (it was opened in 1826), but Graham introduced the modern method in this country. It led in 1845 to the founding of a chair in Practical Chemistry and to the building of the Birkbeck Laboratory.

Opened in January 1846, the new Laboratory was partly financed by money raised to commemorate George Birkbeck's services to the widening provision of education. With bench accommodation for twenty-four students, each place with gas and water laid on, it was pronounced 'the most perfect of its class in the kingdom' by the *Illustrated London News*. George Fownes, the newly-appointed Professor of Practical Chemistry, had studied under Liebig in Germany, and had a number of advanced features incorporated in the design. Fownes published some papers on fermentation and a *Manual of Chemistry* that was to go through eleven editions, but he died young in 1849. The beginnings of practical chemistry were developed by his more famous sucessor Alexander Williamson (see p. 80). When Fownes died, the *Lancet* said the College 'could ill afford to lose so good a man', and declared that death 'seems to second the efforts which intrigue had so successfully commenced for the destruction of this once flourishing institution'. It was a premature judgement.

The Birkbeck Laboratory was designed by Thomas L. Donaldson, the Professor of Architecture since 1841, and architecture must find its place alongside engineering and practical chemistry as the significant developments of the 1840s. The Chair of Architecture was the first to be founded in a university, and Donaldson, who held it until 1865, was an established architect of repute, as well as an outstanding draughtsman and lecturer. He played a leading part in the foundation of the Royal Institute of British Architects, becoming known as the father of the architectural profession in Britain.

88. Thomas Graham, FRS, Professor of Chemistry, 1836-55, and later Master of the Mint, where he was responsible for the change from copper to bronze coinage.

89. George Fownes, FRS, Professor of Practical Chemistry, 1845-49.

An important addition to the life of the College in 1849 was the opening of University Hall in Gordon Square, intended to 'provide for students ... the accommodation and social advantages of college residence'. The Hall was built by the Unitarians in commemoration of the Dissenters' Chapels Act of 1844, 'the first recognition by the legislature', as an inscription on an interior wall originally proclaimed, 'of the principle of unlimited religious liberty'. It was also to be a place where theology, excluded of course from the College, could be taught, 'disavowing all denominational distinctions...' The first Principal was the highly eccentric F. W. Newman, the brother of Cardinal Newman and Long's successor in the Chair of Latin. He resigned before the opening and was succeeded by Arthur Hugh Clough, the poet, who for three years held the Chair of English. Clough had resigned his Oxford fellowship out of religious scruple, but found himself unhappy both at the College and at the Hall, and he too soon resigned. Later distinguished principals included E. S. Beesly and Henry Morley (see pp. 79 and 108). From 1853, the building was shared with Manchester New College, an institution which had its origin in the well-known dissenting academy at Warrington in the eighteenth century, but which migrated to London to be close to UCL. In 1889 it moved on again, this time to Oxford and, under rather odd circumstances, the Hall was then lost to the College and the lease sold to Dr Williams's Library. In 1949 the College acquired the freehold, but the lease does not expire until 2850. The rear annexe, built while Henry Morley was Principal and subsequently named after him, has since 1930 been in the possession of the College, and is occupied by the School of Library, Archive and Information Studies.

90.

91.

90. University Hall, the present Dr Williams's Library, designed by Donaldson as the first hall of residence for the College, at the time of its opening in 1849.

91. The General Library, also designed by Donaldson and now named after him, built in 1849 with aid of a bequest from Jonathan Brundrett on the site of the unfinished original Great Hall which had been destroyed by fire in 1836.

92. Thomas L. Donaldson, the College's first Professor of Architecture, 1841-65, as shown on the medal established in his honour by the Royal Institute of British Architects, of which he was a founder.

92.

93.

94.

At University College Hospital in 1846, Robert Liston performed the first operation under anaesthetic conducted in Europe, an event which marked one of the most striking advances in the history of surgery. Present as a student on that occasion was Joseph Lister who was later to revolutionise surgery through his work on infection and antisepsis. Both these were developments that made an enormous contribution to the reduction of human suffering.

Robert Liston was brought from the Royal Infirmary at Edinburgh to be one of the first surgeons at the Hospital when it opened in 1834, and Professor of Clinical Surgery at the College. He was remarkable for his dexterity while operating at a time when speed was the only relief that could be afforded to the patient. It was said the gleam of his knife was followed so instantaneously by the sound of sawing as to make the two actions appear simultaneous. He could amputate a leg in 20 seconds. He began the era of anaesthetics in Britain on 21 December 1846 after hearing of the first use of ether by a dentist two months previously in the Massachusetts General Hospital. The glass for administering the ether during the leg amputation was devised by William Squire, a 21-year-old medical student. After the experience of the Okey mesmerism fiasco, any new attempt at avoiding pain at UCL was regarded with suspicion, but news of the success spread speedily and the innovation was rapidly adopted. 'This Yankee dodge', announced Liston, 'beats mesmerism hollow'.

Joseph Lister was appointed a house surgeon in 1851 after he had taken his BA at the College, but before he had graduated in medicine. In 1853 he left for Scotland, serving as a surgeon in the Infirmaries of Edinburgh and Glasgow and as a professor in both those universities in turn, thus beginning to repay a little of the College's considerable northern debt. It was at Glasgow that he made his revolutionary discovery of the startling effect of the antiseptic treatment of wounds, reported to the BMA in 1867. He was inexcusably passed over for a chair at UCL, but later returned to London to bring distinction to King's College. In 1897 he became one of the first academics to be raised to the peerage.

Despite these clear signs of potential in the Faculty of Medicine, domestic quarrels continued to characterise the place, a particularly memorable one being that in 1848 over Liston's successor. James Syme was so horrified at the 'spirit of dispeace in the College' that after a tenure of only five months he packed up and went back to Edinburgh.

93. Robert Liston, Professor of Clinical Surgery, 1835-47, the first surgeon to perform an operation under anaesthetic in this country in December 1846 at University College Hospital.

94. A replica of the original apparatus used on that occasion for administering the ether, from the collection of the Wellcome Institute of the History of Medicine.

95. The old wooden operating table used in UCH in the early decades, now preserved in the Museum of the Medical School.

96. The College's plaque in commemoration of Lord Lister, OM, a student between 1844 and 1852, later President of the Royal Society and famous for the development of antiseptic treatment.

To record the deeds of the professors in the first decades of the College's existence is easier than to portray the lives of the students. Their dominant feature was that they were too few to start with, and that they got fewer. The 630 of 1829-30 was just exceeded in the peak of the late 1830s after the building of the Hospital, but then went no higher and by 1864-65 fell below 400. This was despite the age limit being set as low as 15 (though some of the earliest students were even younger) and despite there being no entrance requirements whatsoever. Even after the establishment of University degrees the matriculation exam was taken following entry into the College; the degrees were first examined for in 1839 after a two-year course. Since the students were so young, so few and all male, it is not surprising that activities other than lecture-going were, by modern standards, limited.

97.

CURIOSITIES OF COSTUME.

A SORT of academical epidemic has broken out among the medical students at the northern end of the town; and the youths at the University in Gower Street have not only trenched upon the collegiate trenchers, but have assumed the gown, which ill assorts with the paletot of private life. This strange association of the garb of learning with the habits of the medical students as they live, produces a curious effect; and the neighbourhood of Gower Street has been accordingly startled by the appearance that the combination presents.

We have not heard by what authority the assumption of the toga has taken place among the youths of Gower Street; and indeed it requires no less a person than old GOWER himself to come forth and explain the mystery.

97. A be-gowned but dissipated medical student as portrayed by Punch *in 1847.*

98. The distribution of prizes in the Faculty of Medicine as portrayed in the Pictorial Times *in 1843.*

98.

Student societies, however, quickly sprang up, mostly of an earnest Victorian character, but the medical students soon took on many of their later characteristics. 'As far as vulgarity goes', said *Punch* in 1846, 'the concern in Gower Street may vie with the older establishments of the Cam and the Isis'. In 1837 *Punch* drew attention to the medical students who were reported as having assumed the wearing of gowns: 'This strange association of the garb of learning with the habits of the medical students as they live, produces a curious effect...'

J. J. Sylvester was one of the first students to be expelled (for threatening another student with a refectory knife), but he returned as a professor in 1837. In the meantime he had been placed as Second Wrangler at Cambridge, though as a Jew he could not take his degree there. One of the great mathematicians of the century, he became an inspiring but baffling teacher. After four years he left for the University of Virginia, beginning to balance the College's account with that university. However, he did not stay long in Virginia either, returning to England to follow the profession of actuary and ending up as a professor at Oxford.

99. The title page of a College note-book kept while a student by Walter Bagehot, later author of the classic English Constitution (1867) and editor of the Economist.

100. J.J. Sylvester, FRS, Professor of Natural Philosophy, 1837-41.

Henry Crabb Robinson (ætat 86.)

FLAXMAN GALLERY, UNIVERSITY OF LONDON

'Persons respectably dressed', noted a London guide-book in 1834, 'are allowed to see the interior of the University every day'. There would have been little to be seen, however, apart from the dignity of Wilkins's building itself, though after 1837 there was also Westmacott's statue of Locke. But from 1851 there was the large college of casts and reliefs by the distinguished sculptor and artist, John Flaxman, on display in what was established as the Flaxman Gallery. Flaxman, who died in 1826, had no connection with the College himself. The Gallery was the work of Henry Crabb Robinson.

Crabb Robinson was an extraordinary figure who lived to be 91 in 1867, the friend of Goethe, Schiller, Herder, Hegel, Charles Lamb, Wordsworth, Coleridge and Blake, and of a good many students at UCL for some thirty years. Having studied at Jena and been a correspondent of *The Times* in the Napoleonic Wars, he worked as a barrister until retiring in 1828. In that year he bought a share in the College 'as a sort of debt to the cause of civil and religious liberty', and in his absence was elected to the Council in 1835. 'Old Crabb' devoted much thought and effort to the problems of the College throughout the rest of his life, and, as a Unitarian, was particularly associated with University Hall of which he was a leading founder. His breakfast parties became an institution. 'There was little to

gratify the unintellectual part of man', recalled Bagehot. 'Your host, just as you were sitting down to breakfast, found he had forgotten to make the tea, then he could not find his keys, then he rang the bell to have them searched for; but long before the servant came he had gone off into 'Schiller-Goethe' and could not in the least remember what he wanted. The more astute of his guests used to breakfast before they came...'

He regarded as his most memorable act the creation of the Flaxman Gallery, constructed between the Portico and the new General Library added by Donaldson in 1849. Into the Gallery were put the works of Flaxman presented by Maria Denman, Flaxman's sister-in-law and adopted daughter, who had got into financial difficulties until Crabb Robinson came to her aid.

When the Gallery was redecorated in 1922, Tonks produced the large painting, including Crabb Robinson amongst the founders of the college (see 2.); this was originally placed high above the casts under the dome and so was meant to be viewed from below, a circumstance which explains its otherwise curious perspective. After some years of being conspicuously hung in the North Cloisters the painting is now again displayed in its intended place in the Flaxman Gallery, since the careful restoration of the casts in 1986.

The Committee of Subscribers to the fund for preserving the **WORKS OF FLAXMAN** request the honor of the company of ...

103.

106. One of the models by John Flaxman in the College's possession, which now form part of the Flaxman Gallery as reconstructed after the bomb damage in which many of his works were destroyed: the model for the monument to Lord North, Prime Minister, 1770-82, at Wroxton in Oxfordshire.

104.

104. A drawing of a charioteer: many of Flaxman's drawings were purchased after Maria Denman's death and originally displayed in a room associated with the Gallery. They now form part of the College's notable Art Collection.

105. Flaxman's model for the monument to the orientalist, Sir William Jones, in University College, Oxford.

105.

*Yours very truly
John Morris.*

107.

Richard Potter marked a low point in the teaching of science. Although he did conduct experiments, it was in the terms of eighteenth-century optical theory and, as a teacher, he was notoriously weak. 'The apparatus', one student later recalled, 'was as worn out as the professor. It never did what it was expected to do. Magnetic force, for example, would be demonstrated experimentally by holding a needle to what might once have been a magnet, but had ceased to attract, while the professor said, "You see it wants a little helping, gentlemen".'

A Chair in Geology had been planned from the very beginning of the College, but no appointment was made and professors of other subjects offered the teaching until 1841. Thomas Webster then accepted the Chair, but though very distinguished he had done his best work far earlier. A. C. Ramsey, who succeeded him in 1847, was a survey officer with the Geological Survey and a far more successful professor, but he resigned owing to pressure of other work after four years. Thus John Morris, who stayed from 1853 till 1877, was the first to build any tradition in the subject; it was he who started field-work; the geological museum was founded as a result of gifts in 1855; and the Chair itself was partly endowed under the will of Morris's friend James Yates (see p. 118) who also left a collection of specimens to the museum.

George Grote had been, at 33, the youngest member of the original Council, though his connection with the College had been severed abruptly over the appointment of a minister of religion, J. Hoppus, to the Chair of Philosophy in 1830. It was only resumed in 1849 when he was re-elected to the Council. In the meantime the young banker and MP had published the early volumes of his *History of Greece* and so become one of the most famous liberal scholars in Europe, far more distinguished than most of the professors. He now played a leading role in the reform both of the University (of which he became Vice-Chancellor in 1862-71) and of the College, where he became Treasurer in 1860 and then President on the death of Brougham in 1868.

The University's reform of 1858 was far from popular with many of the College's professors. It opened University examinations to all comers and thus reduced still further the control of the teachers over the examinations; it also left the University of London without any teaching functions, a situation which was to lead to progressively

more vigorous protest as the century went on. However, the same reform brought a major step forward, through the introduction of degrees specifically in science; science courses had previously simply been part of the Faculty of Arts. The College's own constitution was in turn reformed in 1869 by Act of Parliament. The main purpose of the Act was the abolition of the system of proprietors and share-holders, which had become disused and discredited over the years. The proprietors were replaced by Governors, who had the right of nominating their successors, and Life Governors, who were appointed by the Council.

Grote himself only lived until 1871; his final act for the College was the endowment of the Chair of Philosophy of Mind and Logic; the conditions were characteristic of his principles: 'If therefore any such Minister [of religion] should at any time or times be appointed by the Council to the Professorship of Mind and Logic ... I direct that no payment should be made to him out of the present endowment.' It was the same issue over which he had resigned as a member of the Council in 1830.

110.

109.

111.

112.

UNIVERSITY COLLEGE SCHOOL.

W hether or not Grote was responsible for the revival, there can be no doubt that the late 'sixties and early 'seventies gave clear signs of new-found energy in the College. New benefactors were attracted and new building was undertaken. So far, only the central block had been built and Wilkins's plans for north and south wings had seen no realisation except in the early prints. The School, which had from the beginning proved one of the more successful elements of the enterprise, was occupying a considerable part of the building. The Council reported in 1866 that every room was in constant use and that the School could not be confined within the area allocated to it. Worse, space which the School had long been allowed to use was now needed for science teaching, while the School itself was looking for better facilities for its own physics and chemistry classes.

The answer came from Samuel Sharpe, a notable and wealthy Egyptologist and Unitarian translator of the Bible, who became a member of the Council in 1866. He proposed that the South Wing should be built as soon as possible and gave £1,000 to open the building fund, and later another £5000. The new wing, designed to harmonise with Wilkins's building, was the work of Hayter Lewis, the successor of Donaldson in the Chair of Architecture. It was opened in three stages in 1869, 1873 and 1876. The School gradually moved into its new premises and the space vacated was re-allocated for College use. The Library took over more of the first floor, sharing the new space with Arts, which moved upstairs from the ground floor. This in turn created room for a new Hygiene Laboratory after the creation of the Department of Hygiene and Public Health in 1869.

113.

111. A drawing of the College showing the new South Wing constructed for the School between 1869 and 1876, as it appeared soon after completion.

112. A photograph of the South Wing housing University College School.

113. University College School's device, with its spray of oak and the motto Paulatim, *'Little by little'.*

114.

114. The Headmaster's Room in the South Wing, now part of the Registry.

115. The Monitors' Room in the South Wing.

115.

The next development again began with a gift. Felix Slade was a famous London collector, especially of Venetian glass; his collections form a distinguished part of the British Museum. He died in 1868 and left endowments for three professorships in Fine Art, at Oxford, Cambridge and London. Ruskin was appointed in Oxford, Digby Wyatt in Cambridge, but at UCL it was decided to take the opportunity to raise further funds and establish a new School of Fine Art for the teaching of professional artists. Further Slade money helped with the project and also set up Slade Exhibitions and Scholarships for proficient students. These benefactions were received in 1870, another building fund opened and Hayter Lewis again prepared plans this time for the North Wing. The first section was completed very promptly and the new department opened in October 1871.

The Slade was an immediate success and had 220 students by 1875; but its expansion then had to be checked for lack of space. The first Professor was Edward Poynter, who had some experience of the French schools and announced in his opening address the principles the Slade was to follow: 'The superiority of foreign artists ... is undoubtedly due to a habit in the schools of thoroughly following out a course of study from the living model...' It was therefore he who set the Slade tradition of working from living models, though his own very academic work was totally remote

116. *Earl Granville as Chancellor of the University of London laying the foundation stone of the North Wing on the occasion of the Jubilee Festival in 1878.*

117. *The North Wing shortly before its completion as illustrated in* Building News *in 1880, showing the stages of the building.*

118. *Felix Slade, whose name is commemorated by the School of Fine Art established through his benefaction.*

117.

118.

from later developments.

The completion of the North Wing needed another appeal in 1878; this was launched in conjunction with the celebration of the College's Jubilee, at which the foundation stone of the extension was laid and an ambitious statement of the College's requirements issued. Completed by 1881, the Slade occupied the first floor and some of the ground floor, Physiology the top floor and Chemistry the basement, while Zoology moved into the first stage of the building, which the Slade had just left. The twelve years between 1869 and 1881 had seen both the North and South Wings added to the College, but not fully paid for; the College had had to borrow money and its debts became progressively greater.

119.

P oynter maintained from the start that men and women could be taught together in the same classes at the Slade – '...except of course those for the nude model' – and the Slade played a key part in the introduction of women to College life. The *Annual Report* noted with satisfaction as early as 1872 that 'Professor Poynter and his Assistants report that not the slightest inconvenience has arisen from having classes composed of ladies and gentlemen, and the officers of the College are not aware that objections have ever been made by any of the students to this combined instruction'.

The movement for admitting women to the College began with the creation in 1868 of the London Ladies Educational Association, an independent body which organised classes for women and to which UCL professors lectured, the first to do so being Henry Morley and Carey Foster. It may have been the intention from the beginning that this should lead to the opening of regular classes to women students, but the process was very gradual: at first, the women's classes took place off the College's premises; they then moved into College, but the Association not the College was the responsible agent. Finally, it became too much trouble to hold classes separately; the Professor of Political Economy was the first to weaken and lecture to a mixed class. The University opened its degrees to women and by 1878 the Association could be wound up and women students were at last admitted on the same footing as men. Hale Bellot called this the most revolutionary development in the history of the College.

In 1882, a hall of residence known as College Hall was opened for women. Carey Foster and Henry Morley again played a leading role. A year later Rosa Morison, one of the administrators of the new hall, and a strong supporter of women's suffrage, became the 'Lady Superintendent of Women Students' until her death in 1912, when her successor took the less pioneering title 'Tutor to Women Students'.

119. The plaque executed in 1915 by Havard Thomas, then Professor of Sculpture at the Slade, to commemorate Rosa Morison, the 'Lady Superintendent of Women Students' for nearly thirty years after 1883.

120. The original College Hall, the first hall of residence for women students opened in 1882. This engraving of the building in Byng Place, now the Friends' International Centre, shows it as it was in 1834 as the Unitarian Coward College, a precursor of halls of residence.

120.

121. Henry Morley, the indefatigable Professor of English, 1865-89, and one of the leading figures in all developments of the College in the late nineteenth century.

The hero, as opposed to the heroines, of this story was Henry Morley who was indeed one of the most energetic and sympathetic College figures of this period. He had come to UCL from King's as Professor of English in 1865, with a reputation already established by his *English Writers*, a massive survey of English language and literature. Apart from up to twenty hours a week of teaching in College, he lectured generously for Ladies' Educational Associations all over the country, for schools and for the Royal Institution. In 1882 he became Principal of University Hall and was the founder in 1884 of the University College Society, the forerunner of both the Union and the Old Students' Association. As editor of *Morley's Universal Library*, he pioneered cheap reprints of the classics. His nickname, Professor More-and-Morley, was hard-earned. There is no denying the success of his classes or the devotion he inspired in his pupils, but it has to be remembered how isolated his success was in the Faculty of Arts in these years. The great advances in the late nineteenth century were almost all to be in Science and Engineering.

The dominant figure in science in the mid-century was Alexander Williamson. He succeeded Fownes in the Chair of Practical Chemistry in 1849, and united both chairs in the subject from 1855 until 1887. He suffered great physical disabilities, being paralysed in one arm, blind in his right eye and myopic in his left. When he came to UCL, he was already in touch with the leading continental centres of research and theory: he was a professed follower of Auguste Comte, and had studied with Liebig at Giessen. The accepted theory of etherification at the time was that ether was formed from alcohol by the loss of water. Williamson was able to show that the relationship had rather to be one of substitution than of the addition or loss of water; i.e., he postulated a process of continuous atomic exchange, in which the atoms and molecules were conceived of as in motion rather than static. It was a masterly piece of research and made Williamson's reputation when presented to the British Association in 1850. His period of productive research then came to an end. He became instead a considerable College figure, and was largely responsible for the introduction of separate science degrees in the University and for the creation of the College Faculty of Science in 1870. He also built up his foreign connections and was for many years Foreign Secretary of the Royal Society.

122. The first of many suggestions for 'filling the gap' after the completion of both the wings, as presented in Building News *in 1881, showing also a plan of the chemistry laboratory built for Williamson.*

123. Alexander Williamson, FRS, Professor of Chemistry, 1849-87.

UNIVERSITY COLLEGE, LONDON,

122.

124. The five Japanese noblemen who first came to London in 1863, four of whom stayed to study at University College. They are from left to right: Bunta Inoue, Endo Kinsuke, Nomura Yakichi, Yozo Yamao and Ito Hirubumi. Apart from the importance of the individuals shown, the photograph is interesting in itself as the earliest to show any group of University College students.

125. Each of the students of the Satsuma class, who came to University College in 1865, appears on this monument in Kagoshima.

126. Sir Ernest Satow (1843-1929), a University College student who graduated in 1861, as presented in a Spy cartoon.

Williamson in his later years acted as host to some of the earliest Japanese students ever to reach the West, in the period before foreign travel from Japan was legalised. The very first of these students reached London in July 1863 and stayed in Williamson's house as well as registering for his classes. All five later played important parts in the development of the new Japan after the Meiji restoration of 1868 and one of them, Ito Hirobume, eventually rose to be Prime Minister. He and Bunta Inoue (who seems never to have registered for courses) returned after a year, but the three others stayed longer and were still studying when a second group of thirteen students arrived from Kagoshima, where the importance of their visit is still recognized in the form of a monument.

The flow of students from Japan continued throughout the century and into the twentieth, one of the most influential being Joji Sakurai, who studied with Williamson from 1876 to 1881, and who later became the originator of scientific research in Japanese universities. His achievements were recognized by the College in 1937, when he became the first foreign fellow of the College.

Not so recognized by the College was another student of the period, Ernest Satow, who had been a University College student in 1859-61, and became the first Englishman to speak and write Japanese and who also played an essential role in establishing contacts between Japan and the West. Only in 1989 has Satow's importance been belatedly acknowledged by the creation of a Satow Chair in Japanese Law.

In fact, all these many early connections between UCL and the opening up of Japan to Western culture were largely forgotten after the 1940s; now, however, visits have been exchanged to mark the importance of UCL's role in Japan's relationship with the west.

83

127.

semi-circular lecture theatres. Before this, the professor certainly had some equipment, but the teaching had been by means of lectures and demonstrations. Now for the first time experimental teaching, as in Chemistry, was offered to the individual student. Here again, UCL was the pioneer of new methods in England. The example was to be followed in many other science and engineering subjects in the College in the subsequent years. Despite this early start, the facilities for physics remained very restricted until 1893, when the new laboratories called after Carey Foster were opened at the back of the main block. They remained in use until they were destroyed by bombing in 1940. Their site, still at the time of writing covered by 'temporary' post-war huts, is only now being re-developed.

Carey Foster himself was remembered as a modest man, who published relatively little. He is now chiefly remembered for the 'Carey Foster Bridge', a very much more accurate variation of the Wheatstone Bridge. But he was a great influence as a teacher and organiser and laid the basis on which subsequent achievements in physics have been built. His last service to the College was to be the first Principal, after his retirement as Professor, an office created in 1900 and held by him for four demanding years.

Richard Potter's work in what had been called 'natural philosophy' was shared after he retired in 1865 between T. A. Hirst and Carey Foster as Professors of Mathematical and Experimental Physics respectively. In 1867, Hirst succeeded De Morgan in Mathematics and Carey Foster became Professor of what was now called Physics. His great achievement was the introduction of the systematic teaching of experimental physics to students. The original 'Physical Laboratory' was created by clearing out the level space at the top of the seating in one of the

127. G. Carey Foster, FRS, the effective creator of the Department of Physics as Professor between 1865 and 1898, and subsequently the first Principal of the College, 1900-04.

128. The Carey Foster Laboratory opened in 1893, with All Saints' church, later the Great Hall, behind it, showing also the semi circular lecture theatre and the General Library as Donaldson built it.

129. Holtz's Electric Machine, constructed in the Department of Physics in 1869 by William Grant, a mechanic of outstanding ability, Carey Foster's long-serving assistant, his name appearing on the base (inset).

128.

WEGRANT
1869

130.

establish physiology as a subject in Cambridge and was succeeded at UCL by Burdon Sanderson. In 1874, when Sharpey retired, Burdon Sanderson combined both chairs until he in turn left to establish physiology, this time at Oxford, in 1883. Then a third of Sharpey's pupils took over the Chair – E. A. Schäfer, later Sir Edward Sharpey-Schafer, a name he somewhat confusingly took in honour of his teacher. These men virtually created physiology as a research subject in this country.

Burdon Sanderson's years at UCL saw a transformation of the whole position. In 1871 physiology – with some pressure from T. H. Huxley as external examiner – became a compulsory subject for all medical students, and laboratory facilities then had to be expanded to deal with the extra numbers. In 1873, the Chair received its own endowment from T. J. Phillips Jodrell, a wealthy eccentric, so that Burdon Sanderson became the first Jodrell Professor.

A landmark was the creation of the Physiological Society. Its first meeting was in Burdon Sanderson's house and it retained close connections with the College. Originally brought into existence by way of self-defence against the active anti-vivisectionist movement of the 1870s, it subsequently became a link between physiologists working in different parts of the country and a clearing-house for ideas and research. Burdon Sanderson's own research was on problems of cardiac function and in particular the contraction of the heart and all the accompanying phenomena. This was to be a major research area in the Department for many years. But perhaps his most significant contribution lay in the introduction of experiment as a central part of the student's education and in the development of the laboratory facilities which this required. By the time he left, the new accommodation for Physiology at the top of the North Wing was open. His actual teaching was less distinguished; he was notoriously absent-minded and far from lucid as a lecturer. A pupil looking back in 1905 recalled that his eccentricities 'invested what he did with something of the same charm that the conjuror arouses in juvenile spectators, and we were in a state of suppressed excitement based on the uncertainty as to what Dr Burdon Sanderson might do next'.

Physics was a pioneer in adopting modern teaching methods, but it was really only Physiology that rivalled the distinction of Chemistry in its contribution to nineteenth-century scientific knowledge. Pupils of Sharpey dominated the subject and began to colonise other universities and found new departments. Michael Foster became Professor of Practical Physiology while Sharpey still held his Chair in 1869. In that same year, he and T. H. Huxley gave the first practical courses ever offered in biology; in 1870, Foster went to

131.

130. *The Spy cartoon of Sir John Burdon Sanderson, FRS, Sharpey's successor in the Chair of Physiology.*

131. *Sir Edward Sharpey-Schafer, FRS, Burdon Sanderson's successor as Jodrell Professor of Physiology, 1883-99, as stylishly portrayed on the prize medal established in his memory.*

132. *A late nineteenth-century view of the Anatomy Museum, an important part of the teaching of medicine.*

132.

133. Sir Ray Lankester, FRS,
Professor of Zoology and
Comparative Anatomy, 1874-91,
shown by Spy in genial discourse
with a hornbill, overheard by a
fossil fish cephalaspis. 'His
religion', said Vanity Fair, 'is the
worship of all sorts of winged and
finny freaks'.

134. The very fine drawings on the
blackboard and on posters used by
Lankester in his lectures: some
were inherited from Grant, some
done by Lankester himself and
some were the work of Edwin
Goodrich, a young student at the
Slade who was later to occupy
Lankester's Chair of Zoology at
Oxford.

Zoology too found a major research scholar as its professor in 1874 and it too received an endowment from Jodrell, though sadly the donor became insane before he could complete the making of the gift, so that the Masters in Lunacy had to act on his behalf in a complex legal situation. E. Ray Lankester was only 27 when he took the chair, having previously been a Fellow of Exeter College, Oxford. Lankester was a large man, with a massive frame, a mobile expressive face, a booming voice and an impetuous temperament – 'a veritable swashbuckler amongst professors'. He was a dominating figure in his subject, editing the major zoological journal of the period for fifty years and placing his pupils in many of the chairs in the subject at home and in the Empire. He wrote prolifically on a wide range of subjects including fossil fishes, molluscs and arthropods, and in his later years on prehistory and the early history of man.

Soon after his appointment, Lankester introduced practical work into the zoology courses. Once again, with the exception of Huxley's experimental courses, this was an innovation in a British university. It was increasingly becoming a standard part of a science undergraduate's education to receive laboratory experience as an integral part of his course. The practical classes were in this case so successful that in 1879 a laboratory assistant, H. Jessop, was appointed to prepare experiments; his work was pioneering in the running of a zoological laboratory and he was a notable College figure for many years.

134.

In 1891, Lankester returned to Oxford and was succeeded by W. F. R. Weldon, who in fact was to succeed him again at Oxford ten years later when Lankester was appointed as Director of the Natural History Museum. Weldon was one of the first men to introduce quantatative methods into zoology and together with Galton and Pearson (see p. 105) created a new branch of the subject known as biometrics, the statistical study of animals. Weldon's own research, especially on shrimps, was designed to test the theory of natural selection by carefully devised statistical analyses of inherited characteristics.

135. *The students attending one of Lankester's courses in 1887.*

136. *The Comparative Anatomy Lecture Theatre in the first stage of the North Wing vacated by the Slade after 1881.*

137. *W. F. R. Weldon, FRS, Jodrell Professor of Zoology and Comparative Anatomy, 1891-99, whose widow in 1936 left money to establish the Chair of Biometrics in his memory.*

138. *The Zoology Museum in the 1880s, with many of the exhibits which are still in the possession of what is now the Department of Biology.*

138.

139.

139. Daniel Oliver, FRS, Professor
of Botany, 1860-88.

140. Daniel Oliver's son and
successor, Francis Wall Oliver, FRS,
Quain Professor of Botany,
1890-1929.

Three Professors of Botany spanned the whole first century of the College's existence. Daniel Oliver succeeded Lindley, one of the original professors, in 1860, and in 1888 he was in turn succeeded by Francis Oliver, his son, first as lecturer (at 24) for two probationary years, and then as professor for thirty-nine years until 1929. Both Olivers made notable contributions to their subject and advances in its teaching.

Daniel Oliver worked for thirty years primarily as Keeper of the Herbarium at Kew Gardens when it was the world's botanical Mecca. He helped form an incomparable systematic collection of the plants of all continents. He lived at Kew and for twenty-eight years gave his lectures in College every morning during the summer terms at 8 o'clock, which meant being woken by the Gardens night-constable rapping on his window at 5 a.m. He regularly brought with him six different specimens for each of the students to examine. The subject took a major step forward in 1880 with the establishment of its first laboratory in the narrow former Microscope Room in the North Cloisters. Botany became no longer simply a subsidiary subject for medical students, one in which they could often see little point, but a scientific discipline in its own right. Soon after the young Oliver succeeded his father,

he put a plan requiring further accommodation to Sir John Erichsen, the then President of the College, who opened the interview and closed the matter with: 'Mr Oliver, you are a very young man and not the only professor in the College'.

F. W. Oliver began field courses in botany, related especially to his interest in the vegetation of maritime habitats. The pioneer expedition was to the Norfolk Broads in 1903, followed by the first of a series of Edwardian summer visits to Bouche d'Erquy on the coast of Britanny. After 1910 the field courses found a settled home at Blakeney Point in that part of Norfolk which is perhaps the finest stretch of marshland coast in Britain. Oliver was instrumental in having the area preserved by the National Trust so that students could, as he said, 'come face to face with the operations of Nature in its most dynamic form'. A series of Blakeney Point publications followed, and Oliver's approach to the changing relations of habitat and vegetation had a very significant effect on the development of the subject in Britain. Ecology has remained an important interest of the botanists of the College, and Blakeney Point is still in regular use as a field station. Since 1960, there has been a postgraduate Diploma in Conservation (later an MSc course) set up as a result of a joint initiative with the Nature Conservancy. Ecology and conservation were thus matters of concern at UCL long before they became vogue words in the 1970s and after.

140.

141.

142.

143.

141. The first Botany Laboratory, as it was in 1891 in the North Cloisters (looking towards the present cloakroom).

142. The Old Lifeboat House at Blakeney Point.

143. Soil investigations being conducted at Bouche d'Erquy in 1904.

144. The Laboratory at Blakeney Point, Norfolk, built in 1913 for the Department of Botany.

144.

146.

146. A torsion testing machine, built by Kennedy himself, which had been installed in the original Engineering Laboratory housed in the space now occupied by the Lower Refectory.

147. The Drawing Office on the top floor of the Engineering building long desired by Kennedy, soon after its eventual construction in 1893.

148. The single-story part of this building along the Gower Street frontage of the College, before the second storey was added in 1922.

Like Lankester, Alexander Kennedy came to University College in 1874 when he was 27. He stayed fifteen years and then left to start a new career. His achievements in the meantime give him a fair claim to be considered the creator of modern engineering education. At the moment of of his arrival, engineering at the College was in some trouble, both his predecessors having left after short stays for better paid posts. The *Annual Report* of 1874 acrimoniously commented on Kennedy's predecessor's resignation to go to one of the new provincial university colleges, that it 'furnishes an additional illustration of the unequal competition with state-aided institutions to which this wholly self-supporting college is exposed, and which from time to time robs it of able teachers, to the detriment of its usefulness and prosperity'. Despite the low salary (under £200), Kennedy's immediate contribution was to provide new teaching methods and approaches by providing translations of up-to-date foreign research.

More significantly, he followed the lead of Carey Foster in establishing laboratory work as a fundamental part of undergraduate education. By the time of the Jubilee in 1878, the College had firmly adopted his line and the formation of a new Engineering Laboratory – the term itself being new – was one of the objectives of the Appeal. Space was provided in the main building and, with a small grant and much improvisation, the pioneering laboratory which was to serve until 1893 was established. Kennedy was versatile and restless: he left College in 1889 to found a highly successful firm of electrical consultants – Kennedy and Donkin. In his later years, he wrote on mountaineering and on archaeology; he was knighted and much honoured. It is a measure of his impact on University College that he left three chairs where he had found one: in 1883 a separate appointment was made to the Chair of Civil Engineering and Kennedy limited himself to Mechanical Technology. In 1885, came a completely new and very important departure – Electrical Technology.

Ambrose Fleming was the first Professor of Electrical Engineering, holding the post between 1885 and 1926. He was born in Lancaster in 1849, but educated at UCS and UCL, where he studied physics under Carey Foster and mathematics under De Morgan. He had taught science in schools and at University College, Nottingham, before being offered the new Chair established by Kennedy which he was to hold until he retired at 77; he lived on to be 95.

It is clear that his teaching duties were not over-onerous; for many years he gave one lecture a week on Fridays at 11 o'clock. This gave him plenty of time for wide public lecturing, and for profitable service as scientific consultant to Marconi. It was this connection which led to Fleming's most celebrated achievements. The plans for the first long-distance wireless station in the world at Poldhu in Cornwall, were, he later claimed, drawn on the lecture-table of the Electrical Engineering Department. His key discovery, made in 1904, was the thermionic valve, a revolutionary new technique for receiving high-frequency electro-magnetic waves, which made radio possible and marked the birth of modern electronics. Fleming realised that use could be made of an effect noted by Edison that, if a metal plate is introduced into an ordinary evacuated carbon filament electric lamp, current will flow in only one direction. From this clue, he developed a bulb which would act in relation to electric current as a valve acts in a water-pipe. The system was improved later by others, but Fleming had made the fundamental breakthrough.

The equipment Fleming found when he took his Chair was 'a blackboard and a piece of chalk'. The situation improved slowly, but in 1891 yet another appeal initiated a new building to accommodate the developments in both Mechanical and Electrical Engineering. This is the building, shown on the previous page (*148.*), still used by some Engineering departments, facing onto Gower Street at right angles to the South Wing, beginning the enclosure of the Front Quadrangle. For lack of resources, only a part of the upper storeys could be built, some of the ground floor being left with a temporary roof.

149. Sir Ambrose Fleming, FRS, Professor of Electrical Engineering for forty-five years from 1885, as painted by Sir William Orpen.

150.

151.

150. The thermionic valve as invented by Fleming at UCL, one of the most important inventions of the twentieth century, now on disply in the Department of Electronic and Electrical Engineering.

151. The thermionic valve in its original versions with Fleming's own caption.

Nothing worried the Victorians more than their drains and, in this regard as in others, the College was responsive to the needs of society. Hygiene was at first taught as part of medical jurisprudence, though its most famous teacher, Edmund Parkes – 'the father of hygienic science' – was in fact Professor of Clinical Medicine from 1848 to 1860, before he left to become Professor of Hygiene at the Army Medical School. In 1869 the Council decided, since 'the subject has become so extensive in its developments and applications', to appoint a Professor of Hygiene and Public Health. W. H. Corfield,

one of the leading authorities in the field, held the Chair for thirty-four years, simultaneously holding posts as a Medical Officer of Health and running a large consulting practice. In 1875 he opened the first laboratory in London for the practical teaching of hygiene; this was on the ground floor of the main building where it was to remain until 1908.

When Sir Edwin Chadwick died at the age of 90, he left a large sum in trust 'for the improvement of sanitation'. Chadwick had been Jeremy Bentham's secretary in his last years and, as a leading disciple, played a combative, if not truculent, part in the

152. Sir Ambrose Fleming's Electrical Engineering Research Laboratory, in which the thermionic valve was invented – the room is now used by the examinations section of the Registrar's Department.

153. Engine drives to the electricity generator in the Electrical Engineering Laboratory of 1893.

154.

153.

struggle to achieve satisfactory public health and sanitary conditions. A large collection of his papers is kept in the Library. It was because of the Benthamite connection and the presence of the teaching of hygiene in the College that Chadwick's trustees chose UCL as the home of a new course of instruction for young men likely to become municipal engineers. Both the new Chair of Municipal Engineering and the existing one of Hygiene became Chadwick Chairs.

By a somewhat curious arrangement, the new Chair was first occupied by Chadwick's son Osbert, the chairman of the trustees: he drew no salary and performed his duties vicariously, though he did organise the syllabus and the courses, and did this admirably. The Department of Hygiene was moved to the top floor of the South Wing when the Boys' School moved out, but then medical hygiene left the College entirely in 1929, when it became a major part of the new School of Hygiene and Tropical Medicine. Municipal hygiene, however, was retained in Engineering at UCL. Major research activity in the Department dates from 1930 when a new Chadwick Laboratory was opened thanks to the continued support of the Chadwick Trust. Municipal Engineering and Hygiene remained as a separate Department until 1947, when it was merged with Civil Engineering.

154. The oil vacuum pump originally used by Fleming for evacuating the valves.

155. The Chadwick medal, still awarded for the study of public health, in commemoration of Sir Edwin Chadwick.

156. The Hygiene Laboratory of 1908 in the South Wing.

157. The apparatus of an early experiment in sewage treatment in the Chadwick Laboratory of Municipal Engineering established in the 1890s.

William Ramsay came to University College in 1887 from University College, Bristol, where he had been both Professor of Chemistry and Principal. He had already completed distinguished research, had travelled widely, and made personal contact with most leading contemporary scientists. The research which was to make his a famous name was undertaken at UCL. The physicist Lord Rayleigh discovered that the density of the element nitrogen obtained from the atmosphere was always greater than that of nitrogen produced from its chemical compounds. With Rayleigh's consent, Ramsay set out to provide an explanation. Using the fact that nitrogen is taken up by heated magnesium, he established that the progressive removal of nitrogen from air concentrated in the residue an unknown gas heavier than nitrogen.

The result was the discovery of a chemically inert gas which he called argon (the Greek for 'idle'). Furthermore, Ramsay realised that if there was to be one inert gas then there ought to be a whole group of such gases filling a gap in the periodic table of the elements. In rapid succession between 1895 and 1900 he established the existence of terrestrial helium (the presence of helium had already been detected in the sun's chromosphere during the eclipse of 1868), as well as of neon, xenon and krypton. His successes brought swift recognition; he was knighted in 1902 and received the Nobel Prize together with Rayleigh in 1904.

158. Sir William Ramsay, FRS, Professor of Chemistry, 1887-1913, photographed in his laboratory in the basement of the North Wing.

159. The Nobel Prize awarded to Ramsay in 1904 for his discovery of the inert gases.

159.

R amsay's great discoveries were made in the North Wing basement laboratories that had been built for Williamson in 1881. Williamson had evidently inspired little activity in his last years and a good deal of the space then allocated had not in fact been used. Ramsay's staff at first consisted of two assistants who had, of course, to be paid out of the professor's fees. Later he was able to appoint a student demonstrator. There was no money available for research expenses and indeed Ramsay paid for his own scientific work very largely out of his own consultancies. The Department of Chemistry expanded rapidly from this slender foundation.

In the early 'nineties, the whole laboratory was fitted with working benches and extra space in the basement cleared out. In 1902 a second Chair, in Organic Chemistry, was established and filled by J. Norman Collie, who had been one of the two assistants when Ramsay first came to London. Student numbers increased year by

160.

year; Ramsay was closely involved with their instruction and toured the laboratory twice a day, at least in the early years. He and his wife also established personal relations with students and had groups of them to dinner regularly through the winter. He was also a notable public figure. Before coming to UCL, he had been a leader of the movement to obtain government support for the universities and university colleges, a campaign which led to the first Treasury grant and the origins of the UGC in 1889. He worked for some years in connection with

161.

the Royal Commission on the Disposal of Sewage, and was a leading advocate of the reform of the University of London. He was honoured throughout the world.

Norman Collie, Ramsay's professorial colleague, was involved in his days as an assistant with the development of X-ray photography. In 1882 he had gone to Würzburg in Germany to do his PhD (a degree then not yet introduced into this country), and happened to be there again in 1895 when Röntgen accidentally discovered the remarkable properties of what he called X-rays. Two months later, in February 1896, Collie was back in London and was responsible for taking the first X-ray photograph used for clinical purposes in this country. The subject was a patient at University College Hospital who had a broken needle in her thumb. The use of X-rays for medical diagnosis and for treatment was rapidly taken up after this signal example of co-operation between scientific research and medicine in the College. Within a few years the Hospital had an expanding radiography department.

Collie went on to work with Ramsay on the inert gases and later cooperated in the pioneering work on the 'emanations' of radium, later to be called 'radon', and the decomposition of this into helium. Here they were unquestionably working on the fringes of the understanding of atomic structure, though the most dramatic discoveries were to be made in Cambridge some years later and through different techniques.

162.

160. The working benches in the Chemistry Laboratory in the North Wing as in Ramsay's day.

161. The Department of Chemistry in 1899, one of the earliest surviving departmental photographs, with Ramsay standing in the centre.

162. J. Norman Collie, FRS, Professor of Organic Chemistry, 1902-28, as photographed in his laboratory for the Sphere in 1921.

163. The first X-ray photographs used in Britain for clinical purposes taken by Collie in 1896 and preserved in the Chemistry Department. They show a broken needle in the thumb of a patient at University College Hospital.

163.

166.

ILLUSTRATION OF EFFECT OF A
RELATIONSHIP BETWEEN FERTILITY
& INTELLIGENCE

165.

*164. Karl Pearson, FRS, Professor
of Applied Mathematics and
Mechanics, 1884-1911, and Galton
Professor of Eugenics, 1911-33,
photographed in 1910 with his
beloved Brunsviga adding
machine.*

*165. The Applied Mathematics
Instrument Room as arranged in
1896-97.*

*166. A diagram from Pearson's
papers illustrating the statistical
treatment of human phenomena
which increasingly fascinated him.*

K arl Pearson was one of the dominating figures in the academic history of the College, with interests and enthusiasms ranging across politics, literature, law and science. Of the beginnings of his long and productive association with UCL, he characteristically said: 'Professor Beesly, just because I had lectured to revolutionary clubs, Professor Croom Robertson, just because I had written on Maimonides in his journal *Mind*, Professor Alexander Williamson just because I had published a memoir on atoms, and Professor Henry Morley, just because I had attended and criticised lectures of his on the Lake Poets, pressed me to be a candidate for the Chair of Mathematics!' It was Alexander Kennedy who finally persuaded him to forsake the law and take the Chair of Applied Maths in 1884.

In the 1890s he became more and more interested in applied statistics and the correlation of biological and sociological data. He was captivated by Francis Galton's *Natural Inheritance* (1889) and the beginnings of 'eugenics' based on the conviction that the ideas of Darwin – Galton's cousin – might be applied purposively to improve the human race. In 1901, Pearson, Galton and Weldon founded *Biometrika*, and in 1903 the Drapers' Company funded a new Biometrics Laboratory for Pearson. Soon afterwards Galton founded the Eugenics Laboratory in a Gower Street house, and after his death in 1911 Pearson came to have charge of both laboratories as Galton Professor. An enormous output of research continued on many aspects of intelligence, craniometry, heredity and 'questions of the day and of the fray'. There was a good deal of fray. Originally housed in the South Wing, after 1920 the work moved into the Bartlett Building, appropriately renamed the Pearson Building before the death in 1980 of his son, Egon Pearson (see *383.*).

167. Francis Galton, the creator of 'eugenics' and founder of the Galton Laboratory – one of the pictures in the massive biography 'K.P.' wrote of him.

168. Galton's finger-prints, as appearing on the title-page of the pioneering book on the subject he published in 1892.

169. Galton's pocket recorder of anthropometric information, as displayed in what is now called the Department of Genetics and Biometry, housed since 1968 in Wolfson House across the Euston Road.

167.

168.

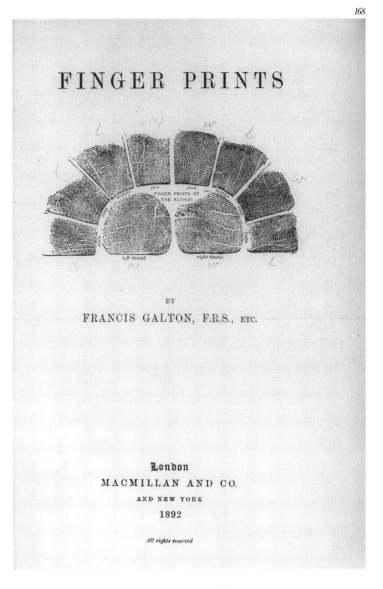

FINGER PRINTS

FINGER PRINTS OF THE AUTHOR

left thumb   right thumb

BY

FRANCIS GALTON, F.R.S., ETC.

London
MACMILLAN AND CO.
AND NEW YORK
1892

All rights reserved

169.

The Revd. T.G. Bonney succeeded Morris as Professor of Geology in 1877 and remained for almost twenty-five years. He came from St John's College, Cambridge, retaining his Fellowship there and originally continuing to teach and live in Cambridge, while commuting to London. Bonney was a vigorous and respected teacher, though the Department remained a small one; he published prolifically and authoritatively, specialising in the study of rocks and in the geology of the Alps. Throughout his years at UCL, Bonney remained a part-time professor; he was a very active Secretary of the British Association for five years and in the 'nineties found lucrative employment writing for a London newspaper.

W. K. Clifford in his brief tenure of the Chair of Applied Mathematics left an enduring impression of quite exceptional abilities. A brilliant mathematician and an original thinker on the philosophy of mathematics, he was one of the pioneers of the conception of non-Euclidian space. His lectures were given with a minimum of preparation beforehand and from the briefest notes. 'The worst of these examinations', he once said, 'is that you have to think what to ask the fellows before you come in, whereas, when you lecture you need not think at all.' His health soon deteriorated and he died of 'pulmonary disease' in 1879 when he was 33. T.H. Huxley regarded his death as one of the greatest losses to science in his time.

170.

171.

172.

GORDON STREET

GORDON SQUARE

GOWER STREET

GOWER PLACE

LITTLE GOWER PLACE

GOWER ROAD

ALL SAINTS' CHURCH

CATHOLIC AND APOSTOLIC CHURCH

TORRINGTON PLACE

University Hall

Dissecting Room

Gymnasium

Cloisters

Cloisters

Library

Class Room

Slade School

UNIVERSITY COLLEGE

Monument

Play

Ground

School

UPPER GOWER MEWS

Lodges

GOWER STREET STATION (Met. Ry.)

POST OFFICE

BEAUMONT PLACE

EUSTON

TOTTENHAM PLACE

SOUTHAMPTON COURT

MAPLE'S

GRAFTON STREET EAST

Ward

Ward

HOSPITAL

HUNTLEY STR.

SHOOLBRED'S

CITY BANK Branch

UNIVERSITY STREET

UPPER CHENIES MEWS

LITTLE PANCRAS STR.

MORTIMER MARKET

PANCRAS STREET

NATIONAL SCHOOL

THE YARD

GOWER STREET EAST

FRANCIS STREET

TOTTENHAM COURT ROAD

173.

170. Revd T. G. Bonney, FRS, Professor of Geology and Mineralogy, 1877-1901.

171. W. K. Clifford, FRS, Professor of Applied Mathematics, 1870-79.

172. A plan of the College as it was in 1887. By this time, both wings had been built, but the South Wing was still housing the School, the fourth side of the Quadrangle was open except for the old lodges, and there was still no development outside the Quadrangle itself.

173. A view of the Front Quad from Gower Street c. 1880.

It is paradoxical that the College's weakest subjects in the nineteenth century were those in which a Benthamite foundation might have been expected to be most creative – history, law, philosophy and economics. The problem resulted from a shortage of students and money, rather than of talented teachers. E. S. Beesly, for instance, Professor of History for over thirty years, was an important figure outside the College. He was a follower and translator of Comte, an active socialist and one of the first British academics to be in touch with the Labour movement, indeed with Marx and the First International. *Punch* honoured him with the nickname 'Professor Beastly'. Crabb Robinson lamented that 'Beesly is going to a meeting of bricklayers

174. E. S. Beesly, Professor of History, 1860-93.

175. G. Croom Robertson, Professor of Philosophy, 1867-92, the first Grote Professor.

176. W. Stanley Jevons, FRS, Professor of Political Economy, 1875-81.

177. An unmistakable failure even on his own view ('I could not help feeling I was scarcely a success') was the Revd A. J. Church, Professor of Latin, 1880-89. His cousin, Sir John Seeley, Regius Professor of Modern History at Cambridge, who had himself held the Chair of Latin in the 1860s, tried to dissuade him from putting in for it since 'as a Christian' he would find his position uneasy at UCL. He certainly met with student protest. The first signatory of the petition against Church's classes was later to become the College's first Provost.

174.

175.

and says they conduct business better than scholars'; a serious attempt to sack him in 1867 was narrowly diverted by Grote. His commitment to his classes, however, was minimal; he used to 'come into his lecture room at 2 o'clock every Thursday, give us one lecture on Ancient History, one on Modern History, put on his comforter and hat; walk out; and that was all we saw of him till next week'.

Philosophy by contrast found a devoted and inspiring teacher in Croom Robertson, despite the bitterness which attended his original appointment (see p.36). Intellectually active, and editor of *Mind* for its first sixteen years, he was a trenchant critic of the existing degree examining system. In Political Economy too

a distinguished professor had little impact. W. Stanley Jevons was a former student of both UCS and UCL, where he had developed his scientific interests; they led him to his pioneering application of quantitative and statistical techniques to economics. Jevons was the first to apply the modern concept of 'utility' in economics. But he found lecturing a great strain and, as his health deteriorated, gave the Chair up after six years. Neither he nor his successor H. S. Foxwell made any significant progress towards the creation of a school of economics at UCL and the foundation of LSE in 1895 was a conscious reaction to the failure of the College to develop the social sciences.

176.

The Council
University College London.

Gentlemen.

We, the undersigned Students of the Faculty of Arts in University College, desire to express our dissatisfaction at the manner in which the functions of the Latin Chair are at present fulfilled, and to respectfully petition that you will endeavour to remedy it.

It is now generally acknowledged, and has been for several years, that the lectures on this subject are scarcely adequate for the Pass Examinations of the University of London.

Those who cannot afford to incur the expenses of private tuition in Latin are therefore obliged to do all their work in that subject by themselves.

The signers of this petition hope that it will not be regarded as any breach of discipline on their part that they should attempt to call attention to a state of affairs which is seriously injuring the College, the more so as they regard Prof. Church in his private capacity with high esteem.

1. Students who are now attending Latin lectures, and desire to express their dissatisfaction.	2. Students who have ceased to attend because they were dissatisfied with the lectures.	3. Students who refused to join the Latin classes owing to unsatisfactory reports.
v J. G. Foster.	v G. J. Hill v	H. Frank Heath
P. Roscoe	W. Rolleston v	Helen Bayes.
J. B. Paysn Payne	v Mary Paul	Horace J. Harris
W. Bournett	Rosa E. Sly.	P. Hope.
A. Hair.	v J. Vodoz,	P. Moon
W. J. A. Butterfield	W. Anderton	D. Rees.
J. A. Onions	A. Paul	7. Duncan
J. V. Thomas.	H. W. Doubleday.	
G. Street	W. June.	
C. H. Vellacott.	10. F. D. Parnther.	
J. H. Morgan.		
12. C. Frederick Bont.		

(22)

University College London.

(Gower Street) 16th June — 1887.

My Dear Sir —

I should have the greatest pleasure in associating myself with my colleagues in honouring the worth and fame of Prof. Williamson who has so well merited of one of the most useful sciences as it is to confer in future the greatest blessings on suffering humanity, and much more so because I entertain a special personal regard for this distinguished Professor himself. But my private means unfortunately prevent me absolutely from taking part in this useful compliment. It is extremely painful to me to state this; but it is only too true that my profession of teacher of the Italian language does not yield the income that it should so that I am obliged to live with the utmost economy and am thus reluctantly compelled to abstain from sharing in those amenities which are the pride of my position, as any unusual outlay however trifling it may seem would derange my household arrangements. From University College I derive no perceptible income, owing to the absence of students who might care to acquire the Italian language, so that next to nothing remains after paying the ordinary fees to and fro. For six years I have also been appointed teacher of Italian in Univ. Coll. School, but during all that time I have not made a clear profit of more than 16/0—! How can I hope for any improvement in the future; on the contrary I have had to undergo an unexpected loss. After having for six years delivered the Barlow lectures on Dante to the great satisfaction of the public who have always honoured me by a numerous attendance, by their approval and applause I had hoped through the favour of the Council to continue the Course in future. Vain hope! Those colleagues of mine who were appointed to make the choice preferred to appoint the Rev. E. Moore of Oxford and I thus lost the little yearly emolument of £30. which I may say was my only income from University College —

Nevertheless I doubt not my more fortunate colleagues will be able without me to pay that Honour to the distinguished Professor which he so well deserves, accepting my good intentions all I can offer under the circumstances. I will therefore ask you kindly to inform the others of the reasons which to my deep regret prevent me from joining in the useful Demonstration.

Hoping with the favour of fortune to have yet an opportunity of doing all I could wish for the Institution to which I have the great honour to belong

I remain

My Dear Sir
Yours very faithfully
A. Farinelli

To Prof. G. Carey Foster
University College
London W.C.

Sep 16.

Cefn-y-Borth,
Rhoscolyn,
Holyhead.

Dear Sir

From your letter, for which many thanks, I gather that the Italian lecturer would have a pretty free hand, and be able to lecture when he liked and as he liked. Students, if any, I presume pay a fee; or is a good conscience his sole reward? There seems to be something of a vicious circle — no students, no pay; no pay, no lectures, no lectures, no students! Still, if I could come at my own time (which would probably be about 5 PM) and were not expected to hold forth more than 24 or so times in the year, nor to give any assistance to young ladies about to spend a winter at Rome, in acquiring a colloquial knowledge of the language, I think I could be of some use. But I am afraid I could hardly afford to work for absolute nothing.

Yours very truly
A. J. Butler

178. A letter from Antonio Farinelli, Professor of Italian, 1880–95, addressed in 1887 to Carey Foster which rather pointedly draws attention to the financial position of many professors at the time. It was discovered in a second-hand book bought in 1977.

179. Another letter written ten years later to the College by A. J. Butler, Professor of Italian, 1898–1910, succinctly drawing attention again to the problems of professorial pay as well as those of teaching languages.

180. Alphonse Legros, Slade Professor of Fine Art, 1875–93, photographed at work.

179

In 1876 the Dante scholar H. C. Barlow died leaving to the College his library, his papers relating to Dante and a fund for the endowment of public lectures on the Divine Comedy. The foundation played a significant part in the development of Dante studies in this country, and it also provided some small (£30) relief for the Italian professor of the day, Antonio Farinelli. He held the lectureship from 1880 to 1886 and, as his recently discovered letter clearly shows, was deeply offended when replaced by the most distinguished Dante scholar of the day, Edward Moore. Farinelli's protests were not quite unavailing, since the College was able to make him a small grant from the Quain fund in 1887. A. J. Butler, who took the Chair of Italian in 1898, was the first Englishman to hold it after a succession of Italians; a distinguished scholar, he took it strictly as a part-time job and with certain reservations, as his letter shows.

The difficulties of the Arts Faculty in this period are illuminated by these two letters. Payment to the professors was still being made, with the exception of a few endowments, on the basis of the number of students who attended their classes. If the class was small, the professor starved. Apart from those who succeeded in attracting large classes and the famous scientists who could supplement their incomes by consultancies, University College professors were effectively part-timers who had to earn their living when not giving their lectures. One improvement had been made in 1868, when a 'Retired Professors Fund' was created for the first time through the generosity of Samuel Sharpe; but the situation over salaries remained unsatisfactory.

The Slade was one part of the Faculty of Arts which proved a great success; it went from strength to strength. Its second professor, Alphonse Legros, came from the world of Paris, and the heart of the realist movement. However, if he came as a new influence in 1876, he fairly soon lost touch with the latest developments in Paris and became an increasingly isolated figure, speaking little English and teaching mostly by demonstration; but the School prospered and expanded in his years, and amongst his pupils were William Rothenstein and Frederick Brown, who succeeded him in 1893 and who admired him as a teacher. All

180.

the same, it is said that as Legros left the college for the last time, he muttered 'Vingt ans perdus'. The College still possesses and prizes a splendid collection of Legros' etchings; as an artist, he seems as yet much under-rated, though he is now receiving his share of the reviving interest in realism.

111

The most significant and influential period of the Slade's history was when Brown was professor and Henry Tonks and Wilson Steer his assistants. It was Brown who discovered Steer's talent as an artist and he who persuaded Tonks to leave his job as a demonstrator in anatomy in a London hospital and join the Slade. The three men were friends and all members of the New English Art Club, the focal point of the most adventurous English artists in the 'nineties. At first, they introduced the ideas of the Impressionists and later developed their own reaction to them. At this stage the Slade was the mediator of the new Parisian methods and ideas; the students who passed through between 1894 and 1914 were to play a leading role in all the new currents in English art up to the 1930s.

The greatest strength of the Slade tradition lay in the variety of talent and technique that it fostered. Brown and Tonks stood for a sort of Impressionism, putting great emphasis on the individuality of the natural object and the artist's response to it; but, not very consistently, they taught a strongly academic tradition, derived from the Old Masters and emphasising structure and proportion in drawing above all else. This core tradition influenced artists as widely different as Augustus John, William Orpen, David Bomberg, Stanley Spencer and Wyndham Lewis.

182.

181. The assembled Slade School photographed in the late 1890s; Brown is just discernable amidst the hats of the Slade ladies.

181.

182. Frederick Brown, Slade Professor, 1892-1918.

183. Wilson Steer, OM, Assistant from 1892 and Assistant Professor, 1922-30.

184. Henry Tonks, Assistant from 1893 and Slade Professor, 1918-30, the third of the great teachers at the Slade in its most influential period.

185. The Slade picnic in 1899. Seated on the horse are, from the left, William Orpen, Augustus John, Gwen John and, with his foot on the shaft, Albert Rutherston. In the waggon are William Rothenstein and his wife, the parents of Sir John Rothenstein, later himself a research student at the College and subsequently Director of the Tate Gallery.

183.   *184.*   *185.*

186.

186. *Augustus John's* Moses and the Brazen Serpent *won the Slade Prize for 1898 and now hangs in the Housman Room. Ambitious but extremely derivative, it shows little sign of his later style.*

187. *Augustus John, OM, a Slade student from 1894 to 1898 and hence one of the earliest of Brown's successful pupils. His legendary talent and iconoclastic life-style made him the very stereotype of the bohemian artist, but he had great influence both on his own and on succeeding generations of Slade students.*

188. *A display of life paintings in the Slade, c. 1906.*

189. *Stanley Spencer's* The Nativity *which won the Slade Prize in 1912, also now in the Housman Room. Spencer had spent four years at the Slade, but this work shows how independently he developed and how mature his style, now so familiar, already was as a student.*

187.

188.

189.

Brown and Tonks were soon left behind by events; they reacted with hostility to the whole Post-Impressionist invasion. Sickert and the Fitzroy circle represented the antithesis of the Slade, but Slade-trained artists like Wyndham Lewis and Edward Wadsworth were in the forefront of new movements. 'What a brood I have raised up' was the austere Tonk's remark about his aberrant pupils. The memories of a contemporary student, Lilian Lancaster, give a vivid picture of one moment in this story of alienation. She and her friend had studied with Sickert and then joined the Slade's classes in 1908 -'serving God and Mammon', said Sickert. 'It is not surprising that this new way of painting caused something of a sensation among the Slade students ... We used to peep through the crack of the door in the rests and saw a number of students crowding round our paintings examining them with great interest, and one day, when I came back to my work, I found "Stipple be damned" scrawled in charcoal in a corner of my canvas'. Miss Lancaster and her friend were discreetly asked to leave at the end of the session.

190.

190. Wyndham Lewis, a Slade student from 1898 to 1901, later the leader of the extreme avant garde in London.

191. Slade ladies painting in the early years of the twentieth century.

192. The Slade picnic, c. 1912, showing Professor Brown (back row third from right) and many students who later became famous: David Bomberg, on Brown's right; Dora Carrington, left of front row; C. R. W. Nevinson, on her left; Mark Gertler, on his left; Edward Wadsworth, in his bow tie and white hat; Stanley Spencer, second from right.

193 & 194. Two more scenes from the famous picnics, one showing Professor Brown with sandwiches.

191.

The first Professor of Classical Archaeology was Charles Newton, a distinguished excavator and one of the founders of the Hellenic Society. He was also Keeper of Classical Antiquities in the British Museum, a post he combined with the professorship. His appointment in 1880 coincided with the height of the aesthetic movement and of the vogue for Greek art, so the new professor's opening lectures on this topic were a sensational success; the fashionable crowds in the Botanical Theatre were led by Oscar Wilde and Lily Langtry. 'But Newton', remarked one of his successors 'never lectured down to his audiences ... and the attendance soon fell to a normal level'. Five years later, the College received an endowment for the Chair. The benefactor was James Yates, an antiquarian and collector who had taken an interest in the College from its foundation – and indeed even earlier, for he had written on the need for a new university in 1826, before he heard of the plans of Campbell and Brougham. When he died in 1871, his will left endowments for Geology and Archaeology, the money to be paid on the death of his wife. Yates's intention had been to regulate the behaviour of his new professor by rules and regulations. 'Another prohibition on which I would insist is that the Professor should not smoke tobacco, not distinguish himself by moustachios, beard or whiskers. He should be a gentleman in manners and appearances and set a good example to his pupils in this and all other things'.

Fortunately, Yates never completed the drafting of these rules and regulations; on these grounds, however, his wife tried to dispute the bequests. There was prolonged litigation on the point and College only eventually won the case in the House of Lords. Newton's successor, R. S. Poole, was again a part-time professor, holding a British Museum post as Keeper of Coins. It was E. A. Gardner, the Yates Professor from 1896 to 1929, who was the first to organise the Yates Archaeological Library and set up a working Department.

195. Sir Charles Newton, the first Professor of Classical Archaeology between 1880 and 1888.

196. The Yates Archaeological Library established with the bequest of both books and money by James Yates.

197. Sir Flinders Petrie, FRS, FBA, the Egyptologist for whom a chair was endowed in 1892, photographed in 1921 with exhibits in the College's remarkable Egyptological collection which he built up.

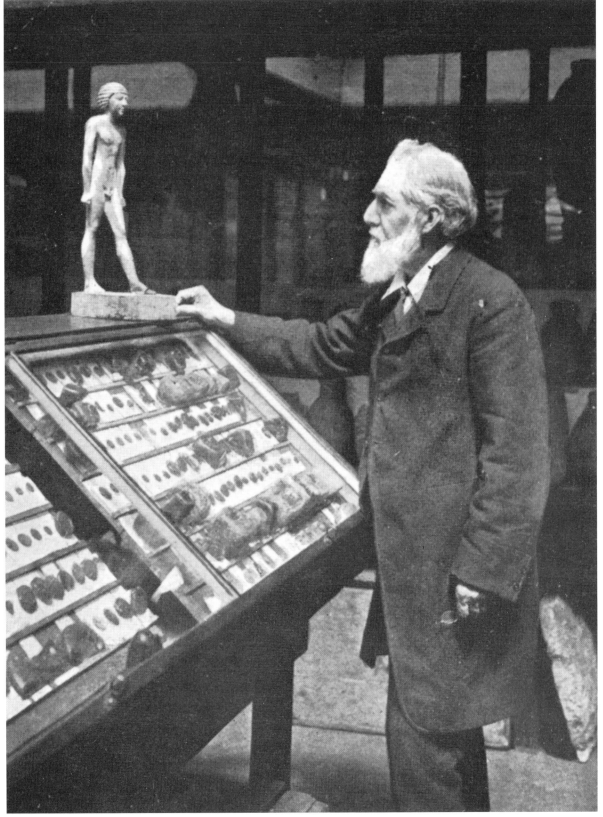

Another bequest started the Department of Egyptology. Miss Amelia Edwards, a novelist and explorer, founded a chair in the subject specifically for W. M. Flinders Petrie. It was her wish that the professor should spend his winters excavating in Egypt; the Department has stood at the centre of the British archaeological effort in Egypt ever since. Petrie's great achievement was to establish the archaeological chronology of Egypt, by collecting and analysing the whole material culture of Egypt, where previous scholars had mostly devoted themselves to art or inscriptions. His collections were eventually acquired by the College and illustrate the long history of Egypt in all its aspects.

Another notable member of the Department in its early days was Margaret Murray, who taught Egyptian hieroglyphics and history at the College for the best part of fifty years, before becoming in her old age a highly controversial figure in the historiography of witchcraft. When over 100, she published memoirs including entertaining, though wildly inaccurate, memories of UCL in the late nineteenth century, including an account of her own part in the formation of a women's common room. Following the desegregation of the senior common rooms in 1969, the former women's common room was re-named the Margaret Murray Room; the name survived until 1989, when the room became the office of the Director of Finance and Planning.

A second great age for the Department began with the appointment of W. B. Emery as Professor in 1951. His digs in Saqqara, the necropolis of Memphis, led to the discovery of the sacred ibises, falcons, baboons and the mothers of the Apis bull. Emery's excavations have been extended by his successors, H. S. Smith, who has worked on the temple complexes of the gods Anubis and Bastet, and G. T. Martin, the present Professor, who discovered the tombs of the General Horemheb and of Tutankhamun's treasurer, Maya. The excavation of the Saqqara necropolis is still continuing, but also, since 1981-82, extensive survey and excavation work in the great city of Memphis itself.

198. Henry Wallis's romantic painting of Petrie excavating at Thebes.

198.

199. A find from the Petrie
Collection: a relief from Koptos of
Sesostris I (c. 1971-50 BC) conducting
a ceremonial dance before the
ithyphallic fertility god Min.

200. Another find from the Petrie
Collection: a portrait of a woman
from Hawara (third or fourth
centuries AD).

201. Margaret Murray, Petrie's
assistant for many years, receiving
an address from the Professorial
Board on her 100th birthday in
1963.

202.

was one of the creators of the honours school of English in the University; and, at the end of his career, he initiated Scandinavian Studies in the College, acting as the first Director of what remained for a long time a unique Department. He was famous for his silences. After his *Dark Ages* was published, Mrs J. R. Green expressed her appreciation of it to him. Ker gazed at her, but said nothing, and did not help the conversation, till she stopped in some embarrassment. After a long pause, he said, 'Go on; I like it'.

Arthur Platt, the Professor of Greek, was very different. He was remembered as the creator of the common-room life of the academic staff, at first using his own private room as a meeting-place after lunch: 'there

The real revival in Arts began with the appointment within a few years of three remarkable scholars: W. P. Ker in 1889, A. E. Housman in 1892 and Arthur Platt in 1894. All three played their full part not only in the intellectual but in the social life of the College and were much in demand as speakers in an age of debates and dinners. Ker, Henry Morley's successor, was to be Professor of English for over thirty years. He published little at first, but his later writings on medieval literature were to have a wide influence. His pupils found him an awe-inspiring figure, full of erudition and of a disconcerting sour wit. Of the three men, Ker was the politician. He

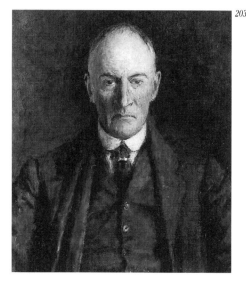
203.

202. A. E. Housman, Professor of Latin, 1892-1911, author of A Shropshire Lad. *This drawing by Francis Dodd hangs in the Housman Room, the senior common room so called in his honour.*

203. The College's portrait of W. P. Ker, FBA, Professor of English, 1889-1922, by Wilson Steer. It is said that the intense quality of the portrait arises from the strong mutual antipathy of artist and sitter.

204. J. Arthur Platt, Professor of Greek, 1894-1925.

he sat for more than a quarter of a century, instructing Chemists in the Humanities and teaching Zoologists wisdom', wrote a colleague – an Arts colleague, of course. He inspired affection in all, including the animals at the Zoo; even the giraffe, a contemporary student recalled, would bend its long neck down and rub its head on Platt's bald pate.

The most famous of the three is, of course, Housman. He had had a chequered early career, having obtained a first in Mods at Oxford, but then failed in Greats. For ten unhappy years he worked at the Patent Office, though for the latter five he was publishing a series of remarkable papers on classical literature. It is one of UCL's claims to glory to have brought him back into the

204.

university world and, when he left after seventeen years, it was to the Latin Chair at Cambridge. His main work was limited in scope to the exposition and textual criticism of Latin poetry – he produced three editions of unsurpassed quality. He struck contemporaries in College as austere and reserved, though all his letters to Platt were destroyed by Mrs Platt after her husband's death as 'too Rabelaisian'. He must have seemed, then as now, a tissue of inconsistencies. There was kindliness beneath the cold exterior, especially towards young people; but he attacked other scholars with extraordinary ferocity. He was a poet – *A Shropshire Lad* was published during his years at UCL – who would write nothing about the beauty of ancient poetry, and devoted thirty years to elucidating the text of a writer for whom he felt little sympathy.

205. Cartoon of an Arts Dinner, showing Ker, Housman and Platt, all regular speakers and 'students crowded to hear them'. The cartoon was the work of R. E. M. Wheeler, a prominent student of the time who attended Housman's lectures; later, as Sir Mortimer, he was to be a famous pioneer both as scientific archaeologist and as academic television personality.

In the second half of the nineteenth century, the Faculty of Medicine was less rent by quarrels and its teaching came to be regarded as unequalled. It had some outstanding professors. Three became baronets: Sir William Jenner, Physician to Queen Victoria and the undisputed leader of the profession at the height of his career; Sir John Erichsen, Danish by origin, Surgeon Extraordinary to the Queen, whose *Science and Art of Surgery* long shaped the teaching of the subject, and Sir Henry Thompson, Assistant Surgeon at UCL from 1856 and Professor of Clinical Surgery, 1865-75, a man of very wide interests, founder of the Cremation Society and of Golders Green Crematorium. Christopher Heath was the last of the great surgeons of the old style: he took to Listerian surgery only under protest, operating in an old frock-coat, turning green, which hung on a hook outside the theatre.

The Hospital itself was by no means as modern as it needed to be, and in 1896 Sir John Blundell Maple, the furnishing shop millionaire, offered £100,000 for its rebuilding. Alfred Waterhouse's design for the new Hospital was arresting, though its red-brick and terracotta Renaissance style was not to everyone's taste; but it was practical in its diagonal cruciform plan from the point of view of ventilation and drainage.

In the end it cost £200,000 but Maple generously paid.

206. The medical staff of UCH in 1897; in the middle are Christopher Heath, the surgeon and Professor of Clinical Surgery, 1875-1900, and Sir Victor Horsley, FRS, Heath's successor, 1900-07.

206.

207.

207. Sydney Ringer, FRS, who entered the College as a student in 1854 and stayed for the rest of his life, serving as a professor in the Faculty of Medicine between 1862 and 1900. He invented 'Ringer's Solution', due to a fortunate accident on the part of a technician.

208. Sir William Jenner, FRS, a professor in the Faculty of Medicine from 1849 to 1879, as sketched by Sir Henry Thompson in 1850.

209. Sir John Erichsen, FRS, another leading figure in late nineteenth-century medicine. He was Professor of Surgery from 1850 to 1877, and President of the College from 1887 to 1896.

208.

209.

210. The bust of Sir John Blundell Maple who financed the complete rebuilding of the Hospital between 1898 and 1906.

211. The old Hospital seen across the tennis court in front of the College.

212. The new Hospital at the time of its opening in 1906.

213.

213. Marie Stopes in sensuous pose while a lecturer at the College. A notorious figure in the social revolution which sought to free women from the miseries of sexual ignorance and haphazard reproduction, Marie Stopes managed to take her First in botany in 1902 after only two years at the College, and her PhD at Munich after only two years more. She returned to UCL in 1911 as lecturer in palaeobotany under F. W. Oliver, holding this post until after Married Love was published in 1918, following which she sought a wider stage.

A great sensation for several years in the first decade of the twentieth century was the 'Brown Dog Affair'. It all began in May 1903 when Stephen Coleridge made a widely-reported speech to the National Anti-Vivisection Society accusing William Bayliss, a teacher at UCL since 1888, of having carried out cruel and illegal experiments on a dog without anaesthetic in the Physiology Laboratory at the College. He had given a lecture showing an experiment involving a dog, which was already anaesthetised for research on pancreatitis and diabetes being carried out by Ernest Starling, the Professor of Physiology. The lecture was attended by two Swedish ladies, active in the anti-vivisectionist cause, and their very garbled account was the basis of Coleridge's absurd charges against the College: 'into its dark portals there passes a never-ending procession of helpless dumb creatures ... into a scene of nameless horror...' Sir Victor Horsley, the UCH Surgeon, and Starling, encouraged the wealthy Bayliss to bring a libel case, and amidst much publicity, he won it. It was clearly established that the dog had been humanely treated and that the experiments were necessary and legal; Bayliss won £2,000 damages which he at

214.

214. Sir George Thane, Professor of Anatomy for forty-two years of blameless service to the College between 1877 and 1919, commemorated by the naming of the medical sciences library after him. He was best known outside the College for his editions of Quain's Anatomy, originally written by two of his predecessors in the chair.

215. The photograph of the reconstruction of Bayliss's lecture used in the famous 1903 libel case. Bayliss – later Sir William Bayliss, FRS, Professor of General Physiology, 1912-24 is on the right, with Professor Ernest Starling and Sir Henry Dale on the left.

216. A postcard issued by the National Anti-Vivisection Society showing the Brown Dog statue at Battersea.

217. A press photograph of the police guarding the site of the Brown Dog statue after its removal in 1910.

216.

once donated to the College for the furtherance of physiological research.

The matter, already a *cause célèbre*, did not end there. The anti-vivisectionists arranged for a statue of the 'Brown Dog' – as the Press had named the creature – to be mounted on a drinking fountain in Battersea. This was put up in 1906. With its insulting inscription referring to the laboratories of UCL, it was naturally found offensive in a College justly proud of the various pioneering laboratories it had built up during the previous generation. The students especially rose to the provocation, and in 1907 there was an attempt to knock the statue down which resulted in ten medical students being fined. Marches, bonfires and other riotous demonstrations ensued, as well as a vigorous correspondence in *The Times* and the *British Medical Journal*. Eventually in 1910, while the College was still taking legal advice, Battersea Council had the statue removed, though the site was for some time afterwards guarded by the police. The outcome of the affair, so far as the anti-vivisectionists were concerned, was a loss of credibility, while according to the Secretary of the College at the time, Walter Seton, this was the first time that the students of different colleges of the reconstituted University had united in support of a common cause.

This is a picture of the Memorial erected at Battersea to the Brown Dog vivisected in the laboratories of University College, London, in 1902-1903.

The evidence of the vivisectors themselves, in the trial of Bayliss *v.* Coleridge, proved that a deep wound was made in the body of the dog in December, and a duct in its inside was tied up so as to deprive it of the proper use of one of its internal organs. The wound was then sewn up and the dog having recovered from anæsthetics it was kept in a cage from December to February. Then a fresh wound was made in its body to ascertain whether the tying of the duct had produced inflammation or not. This was done under anæsthetics, then the dog, with this wound clamped together with iron forceps, was handed over to another vivisector, who fastened it down to a board and made another severe wound in its neck, exposing a gland; he fixed little pipes to the end of its arteries, he attached electrodes to its dissected-out nerves, he put a tube into its severed windpipe which was connected under the floor to an automatic pump in another room, in the charge of a laboratory boy, supplying artificial respiration of anæsthetics, on which apparatus depended the dog's insensibility. After about an hour on that board the dog was finally handed over to a third operator, who killed it.

Men and women of England, how long shall these things be?

THE NATIONAL ANTI-VIVISECTION SOCIETY, 92, VICTORIA STREET LONDON S.W.

217.

Students had long been forming societies for literary, scientific and debating purposes, and from 1858 there was a Reading Room Society. The Union, and hence a coherent structure for clubs and sports activities, grew out of the University College Society founded by Henry Morley in 1884 and open to teachers and students, past and present. In 1890, a separate Old Students' Association was founded and three years later the Union emerged to take over the UC Society's responsibilities for current students and for sports facilities.

The step did not at first arouse the enthusiasm of the College authorities. It was preceded by radical agitation, particularly about the inadequacies of the sports grounds and bureaucratic obstructions by the College Office. A brief but spectacular contribution was made by *The Privateer*, a journal edited by E. V. Lucas, which began and ended in 1892-93. Towards the end of 1892, a committee chaired by Edward Schäfer, the Professor of Physiology, put a proposal up to the Council for a 'combined athletic and social union'. By June of the following year, the Council had not given its consent but at a student meeting a constitution was adopted and a provisional committee set up. The Council then gave its retrospective blessing and from this point on the new Union seems to have received full support from the College. It was given control of three student rooms and began its first session in October 1893, with Schäfer as its first – rather reluctant – President. Not until 1903 was there a student President.

For the seventieth anniversary of the College in 1897, the Union proposed a number of celebrations which became the first Foundation Week. Besides the sports, a concert in the Botanical Theatre, a Union dance in the Holborn Restaurant, there was the first Oration: given by G. Vivian Poore, one of the Professors of Medicine, it was a lively and well-received survey of the history of the College. Foundation Week has been a regular feature of the College ever since.

Orations to celebrate the 150th anniversary were given in both 1977 and 1978 by Sir Harold Wilson and A. J. P. Taylor respectively.

218. The Lounge of the Union in its early years.

219. One of the earliest team photographs owned by the Union: the UCL Cricket Club First XI in 1906 – seated on the ground to the right is E. N. da C. Andrade, later Professor of Physics (see 383.).

220. Another early Union photograph: the Joint College and Hospital Hockey Club in 1906-07 – seated in the middle, as President, is Sir Victor Horsley, the famous neurosurgeon.

218.

219.

220.

Another event significant in the College's history, if on a rather different plane, was reported in March 1900 in the *University College Gazette*, which had been revived in 1895 as the Union's record of events. 'The students then filed into Gower Street, and marched round the Hospital to the tune of nothing in particular admirably rendered by the bugles and penny whistles. A Scott's Emulsion van which happened to drive into the quadrangle at this moment was filled to overflowing, and escorted round the neighbouring streets by numbers of those who didn't succeed in getting in. The sound of an adjacent piano-organ was the signal for a further expedition, and both the organ and its unwilling owner were gently propelled through the College gates ... An exploring party in Tottenham Court Road seized the famous Highlander, and placed him in the post of honour on the Portico – he was soon joined by a representative of the Army, who had been carried to the College on the shoulders of an enthusiastic crowd.' There followed a procession to the West End in a large festooned cart lent by Sir Blundell Maple, a rendition of 'Rule Britannia' outside the War Office and finally a bonfire in the Front Quad.

The occasion for the rejoicing was the relief of Ladysmith by Sir Redvers Buller during the Boer War. The 'famous Highlander' was Phineas Maclino, a large wooden tobacconist's sign, who stood outside Catesby's in Tottenham Court Road. From this occasion onwards, he was repeatedly commandeered for rags, riots and celebrations. In the course of time, Phineas came to be a resident of UCL, if a somewhat erratic one, as the College mascot. He has frequently been the victim of raiding parties from other institutions, but is now in the Union's safe-keeping, sprucely re-painted by Slade students in the mid-1980s, and proudly displayed in the Steve Biko bar.

221.

222.

224.

225.

221. The Union's crest, with the College motto: 'let them all come and receive the rewards their merit earns'.

222. Phineas Maclino, the College mascot.

223-227. A number of snap-shots showing the commandeering of Phineas on Ladysmith night in 1900, and the patriotic scenes leading up to the bonfire in the Front Quad which were enthusiastically undertaken by the students and by the boys from the School.

226.

227.

228.

229.

230.

*228. The only known photograph
of the Council Room as it was in
the late nineteenth century.*

*229. The General Office as
established in 1908, when the old
Office was allocated to the Provost,
who had previously made do with
the Council Room when not
otherwise in use.*

The College's situation at the end of the nineteenth century was far from secure. Building developments had led to a debt of £30,000 which the College had no way of paying off. The salaries of professors were in general inadequate and they had no proper means at all of financing their research. Moreover, the administration of the College had not succeeded in keeping pace with its expansion, though the College was in fact on the verge of a great leap forward in terms of student numbers, buildings and research. Meanwhile, University reform had been under discussion for many years and this was to affect UCL's development in a radical way. From the 1880s there was a strong campaign to promote a 'Teaching University', examining still being the University of London's only function. The solution arrived at in 1898, after two Royal Commissions and innumerable set-backs, was that an organic connection should be established between the teaching College and the degree-giving body. The teachers were given representation on University committees and on Boards of Studies set up to control the various subject areas, while the students were to be required to complete courses of study in the colleges if they were to take 'internal' degrees. UCL wanted to go further than this. It proposed that the College and all its assets should be vested in the University and that all its activities should be carried out under the University's authority. Eventually, after the Drapers' Company paid off virtually all the College's debts, this plan was given effect by the University College (Transfer) Act of 1905.

*230. The College Servants'
Association on one of the earliest
annual outings in the 1890s.*

*231. An unfulfilled proposal for the
College frontage, published in 1894
by T. Roger Smith, the Professor of
Architecture.*

*232. The cover of the UCL Union
Magazine which succeeded the UC
Gazette in 1904.*

231.

U.C.L. UNION MAGAZINE

Since the ill-starred days of Horner, the College had only had the formal leadership of the President, who chaired the Council, while another member of the Council acted as chairman of the Senate. In 1900 it was decided that there should once more be a salaried head, with the title of Principal, who was to chair the Senate and act as the professors' link with the Council. Carey Foster held the post for four years, in which some of the toughest problems were faced, and was then succeeded by the man who had been Secretary since 1900, Gregory Foster (no relation), while W. W. Seton took over the secretaryship. These two men were to guide the College for a long period of substantial change and development. Gregory Foster had been a UCL student in the eighties (see *177.*) becoming a teacher at UCL and then an assistant in the English Department in the 1890s, and third President of the Union in 1896.

Seton was an even younger man: he had come to UCL on his seventeenth birthday and was only twenty-two when he became Secretary. He too had strong academic interests, particularly in Scottish History and in Franciscan studies. Seton was a dour, hard-working Scot, with a somewhat underdeveloped sense of humour, while Foster was a very popular figure, at least with the students. He insisted on interviewing personally all of them at the beginning of each session throughout his Provostship, an increasingly time-consuming exercise which repaid itself in terms of the regard in which he was held. Gregory Foster was very largely responsible for founding the twentieth- as distinct from the nineteenth-century College.

234.

135

235.

235. The new Medical School being
built; it was ready for opening in
1907.

236. The crest of the Medical
School, with Currie symbolised by
a ship, Sir Blundell Maple by
maple-leaves and medicine by the
snake.

236.

Incorporation in the University meant the separation of two elements of the College – the Advanced Medical School and the Boys' School. Both had therefore to be found new premises away from the College. For this purpose the Faculty of Medicine had to be split, the College retaining the pre-clinical teaching and the new 'University College Hospital Medical School' taking over the advanced courses in surgery and medicine. A site and a building were needed. The site was provided opposite the College on the corner of Huntley Street in 1903 through an anonymous gift. The building was presented wholly by Sir Donald Currie, the founder of the Castle Steamship Company and one of the richest men in England, who gave well over £100,000 to the project. He had had no previous connection with the College or with the area, but his life had been saved by a doctor from UCH. The College, after thanking Sir Donald for his gift, passed a vote of thanks to Dr. Batty Shaw 'for having so successfully interested Sir Donald Currie in the Scheme ...'.

The Boys' School was to move a great deal further way, to the site in Frognal, Hampstead, which it still occupies today. Money was again raised by appeal and the School was re-founded as an independent body. The leavetaking on 25 July 1907 was a solemn affair: '... the School, headed by the Cadet Corps, marched into the College quadrangle, formed three sides of a hollow square, facing the great steps and portico, where a chair had been placed for the Provost, Dr T. Gregory Foster. The Head-Master, supported by Beadle and Sergeant, advanced into the Square, and when the Provost had taken his seat above, read the valedictory address before giving up formally the keys of the School building'. Moving speeches were made about the maintenance of intimate links between School and College, hopes which have found little fulfilment in the years since.

The formal act of incorporation took effect on 1 January 1907. Foster's title was changed to that of Provost in readiness in 1906; now the College was to be controlled by a Committee of the Senate of the University; the College Senate became the Professorial Board and the College itself ceased to have a separate legal existence from the University.

237. *Sir Donald Currie, the wealthy shipowner who financed the new Medical School building, now eccentrically re-named the Rockefeller Building.*

238. *Eric Gill's design for the seal of the College Transfer Commissioners appointed under the 1905 Act of Parliament.*

239. *The new building for University College School at Hampstead, soon after its opening by Edward VII in 1907.*

240.

240. R. W. Chambers, FBA,
Librarian 1901-1922, the creator of
the modern College Library, who
later succeeded Ker as Quain
Professor of English Language and
Literature, 1922-1941.

241. The Science Library as created
by Chambers to the north of the
Flaxman Gallery on the first floor
of the main building.

242. The old Mocatta Library,
destroyed in 1940.

243. The bronze plaque of
Frederick Mocatta in the Library.

244&245. Two parts of the new
Geology Department, set up in the
South Wing vacated by the School
in 1907 – the Mineral and Rock
Room and the Geological Museum.

241.

It is ironical that just seventy years later, in 1977, the College completed the lengthy and expensive business of undoing the effects of incorporation. In 1907 it had been an act of faith in the new order, but only King's followed the lead and the University became instead a federation of independent colleges, so that UCL and KCL found themselves in an increasingly anomalous situation. Since 1977, the College has been once more an independent corporation, with a new Royal Charter. The short-term effects, however, were unquestionably beneficial. The departure of the School and the Medical School enabled a major reorganisation of accommodation to take place. Geology took most of the first floor of the South Wing and began a considerable expansion under E. J. Garwood, who had succeeded Bonney in 1901 and who was the first full-time Professor. Extra space was provided for Electrical Engineering and Applied Mathematics while the Eugenics Laboratory was moved into College from 88 Gower Street. Philosophy was also housed in the South Wing, with the Psychological Laboratory adjoining it.

Perhaps the chief beneficiary was the Library, whose reorganisation is one of the great success stories of the period. When R. W. Chambers was appointed Librarian in 1901, he inherited a rich but disorganised domain, largely consisting of bequests and gifts many of them very valuable and many the collections of the professors themselves. But there had been years of neglect: from 1831 to 1871 there was no proper Librarian and in these years the Library Committee seems hardly ever to have met. There was a printed catalogue, thanks to the generosity of Samuel Sharpe and the efforts of Adrian Wheeler as Librarian between 1871 and 1901, but there was no card-index to facilitate the cataloguing of accessions, no space to store them and no administrative structure.

Chambers had been a pupil of Ker and successor to Gregory Foster as Assistant Professor in 1904; later he was to succeed Ker himself as Quain Professor in 1922. He took over not only to face great problems, but also a profound controversy between those who wished to see the Library develop a single centralised organisation and those who preferred subject libraries under the professor's own control and

242.

243.

244.

hence available for teaching use within the department. Chambers fought from the beginning for the integrity of the Library and the solution adopted conceded his main point; the books were to remain under the Library's control, but be kept in separate though linked rooms, as far as possible one for each main subject. With this plan in mind, the Library was able to use the 1907 reorganisation to the best effect: the area to the south of the Flaxman Gallery became a series of linked Arts libraries, while the area to the north – the old Anatomy Museum – became the College's first coherent Science Library.

A most distinguished accession in 1906 was the library of Frederick Mocatta, the wealthy collector and philanthropist, who left his collection of Jewish books and antiquities to the Jewish Historical Society. They arranged, as a memorial to him, that a library, a museum and a room for the meetings of the Society should be provided by the college: in return, UCL became the permanent home of one of the most important Jewish libraries in Britain.

245.

139

The years after incorporation saw significant steps towards the establishment of sustained research programmes of the type to be increasingly familiar in the twentieth century. Ernest Starling as Jodrell Professor of Physiology played a major role. A medic from Guy's, he had been working with William Bayliss (his brother-in-law) for some years before coming to UCL in 1899. Their collaboration was at first directed to the functioning of the heart and to the analysis of cardiac failure. Then in 1902 they turned to work on intestinal function and rapidly made startling discoveries, leading to the principle of hormonal control mechanisms; they were the first to establish that messages were conveyed by chemical agents, transported in the bloodstream, and Starling himself introduced the word 'hormone' in 1905.

Starling conceived and brought to birth the plans for a new medical complex at UCL involving Anatomy and Pharmacology as well as Physiology, intending to transform both medical education and research in London. The first stage, the Institute of Physiology – a title little to the taste of the Provost, who feared secession – was built in 1909 on what had been the Boys' School playground.

In 1912, through the generosity of Andrew Carnegie, the second stage was added for Pharmacology. Starling went on to evolve a general theory of the regulation of the heart-beat (Starling's law of the heart). His experiences in the first world war left him bitterly convinced of the sheer ignorance of the British ruling classes and he campaigned vigorously for basic educational reforms with a scientific curriculum. He resigned the Jodrell Chair in 1923, but remained in UCL as a Royal Society Professor. He died, ironically enough of a heart attack, at sea off Jamaica in 1927.

246. The Institute of Physiology, built on the former University College School playground, soon after its opening in 1909.

247. The College's portrait of Ernest Starling, FRS, Jodrell Professor of Physiology, 1899-1923 and Foulerton Research Professor, 1923-27.

246.

248.

249.

Before 1897 the College had no playing-fields of its own and teams had to rent pitches in Regent's Park or Primrose Hill, the area where many of the students were accommodated. From 1897 to 1906 the new Union rented a ground at Acton, but by 1905 this had proved too small and 15½ acres were bought at Perivale, which was to be the centre of athletic activities until after the second world war. The Perivale ground was formally opened in June 1908. By this time the Women's Union Society was also looking for a sports ground. It had come into existence owing largely to the efforts of Rosa Morison (see *119*.), who had persuaded the College to provide a Reading Room for women students in the eighties and who became the first President of the new Union when it was set up in 1897. Like the Men's, the Women's Union was responsible amongst other things for athletic facilities and so a ground for the women too became a priority. The problem was solved by buying another 7½ acres adjacent to the men's ground at Perivale. The cost of the two together was £3,600; including equipment

248. University College Hall, Ealing, opened in 1908 as a hall of residence for fifty men students. It was sold after the second world war and the funds donated to the Union.

249. A view of Perivale, the sports ground opened in 1908 and used by the College until the 1940s.

250-252. Three Homeric tableaux from the Bazaar and Fete of 1909: from the top, 'Death and Sleep with the body of Memnon', 'Nausicaa playing ball with her Maidens' and 'Penelope at her loom discovered by the Suitors'. In the first, Death is played by E. A. Gardner, Professor of Archaeology, 1896-1929, and in the third, one of the suitors is Mortimer Wheeler.

253. A view of the scene in the Front Quad during the Bazaar and Fête in July 1909.

250.

251.

252.

253.

and drainage, the requirement of the two Unions by 1909 was £7,000. Fund-raising activities, therefore, took up a good deal of student time in the following years. The great Bazaar and Fete of 1909 lasted for three days, occupying the Front Quadrangle and large parts of the College buildings as well. The programme included a fair, dances, concerts, demonstrations, exhibitions and scenes from Shakespeare, as well as Indian and Homeric tableaux. The whole affair was a great success, raising more than a third of the sum needed.

As early as 1912, there was talk of amalgamating the two Unions, a project which in fact had to wait over forty years. The proposal was roundly denounced in the *Union Magazine* for June 1912, which expressed the hope that 'this futile chatter and the exaggeration with which it is embroidered will cease; as it may endanger the present cordial relations which exist between the two Union Societies'. These pre-war years did, however, see a major development in the provision of accommodation for men students. This had been gravely deficient since 1889, when the old

University Hall was acquired by the Trustees of Dr Williams's Library. A committee was set up with Seton as its secretary and Sir William Ramsay as treasurer, to acquire land in Ealing, about a quarter of an hour's walk from the new athletic ground. It was opened in 1908 with room for fifty students, and extended in the 1920s. Walter Seton continued to take a great interest in the new Hall and was its Warden from 1912 to 1922.

The years before the first world war saw a vigorous continuation of building activity assisted by benefactions. In 1911 Sir Herbert Bartlett, a building contractor, provided practical support for the proposal that the Departments of Architecture at King's and UCL should be merged, by donating £30,000 for the necessary building. The benefaction was also intended to provide for the accommodation needed by Karl Pearson's department; the whole building would provide a north-west frontage on to Gower Street. Almost complete by the outbreak of war, it was first used as a temporary war-time hospital under the management of UCH.

254.

255.

254. *The set built by F. M. Simpson, the Professor of Architecture, in one of the old semi-circular lecture theatres, as used in 1907 for the production of the Greek plays which were a feature of the years about the turn of the century.*

255. *The programme of events at the three-day Bazaar and Fête of 1909.*

143

256.

258.

259.

The other major benefaction on the eve of the first world war provided expanded accommodation for the work of the Department of Chemistry. Sir William Ramsay's successor as Professor of Chemistry was F. G. Donnan, a distinguished physical chemist, who had first come to UCL to work in Ramsay's laboratory in 1898, and subsequently held posts in Dublin and Liverpool before his return in 1913. He is now best remembered for the 'Donnan membrane equilibrium', concerned with the transport of ions and molecules across the living cell. By the time he took over the Department, the building of the new laboratories, facing Gower Place and extending the College site northwards, was already well advanced. Much of the money was given in 1911 by Sir Ralph Forster, whose bust remains in the entrance hall; a closing order was obtained for Little Gower Place in 1912 and the impressive building, designed by Simpson, was in use, though not finished, by 1915.

259. Sir Herbert Bartlett, whose generosity made the building possible and whose name is borne today by the School of Architecture and Planning in Wates House, where his bust remains.

260. The new Chemistry Laboratories facing onto Gower Place, first opened in 1915 (now housing the Sandoz Institute for Medical Research).

261. A cartoon inspired by a remark of F. G. Donnan, FRS, Professor of Chemistry, 1913-37: 'The lifeblood of England is sulphuric acid'.

261.

262. The College's work continued during the war, though the number of students declined sharply (see p.231). A high proportion never returned; no less than 301 members or former members of the College were contributed to 'the lost generation'. Here Armistice Day is being commemorated in the Front Quad in November 1922, by the memorial inscription placed in front of the Portico; the Roll of Honour was read out by the Provost and the Dean of the Medical School, and the Librarian received the first volume of the War Memorial Album. In the background can be seen the addition to the College buildings opened in 1920 by Lord Addison, the first Minister of Health, after its use as a war-time hospital annexe; Sir Herbert Bartlett by then had been revealed as the donor, and his name was given to the new School of Architecture.

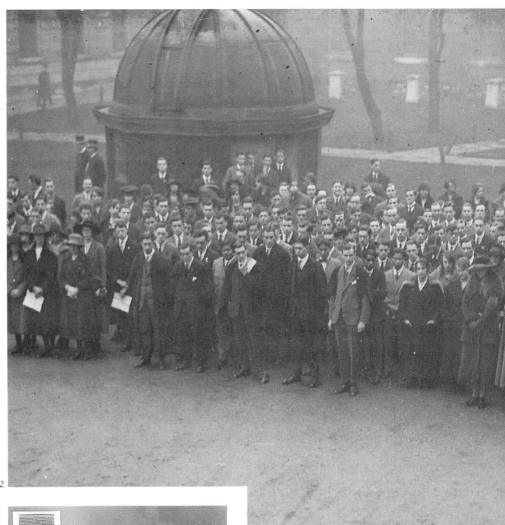

262.

263. The first man to win the VC twice – Arthur Martin-Leake, a graduate of the Faculty of Medicine: he won it first in the Transvaal during the Boer War in 1902 and then again in France in 1914.

263.

264. A cartoon from the University College Union Magazine *of 1915, showing the way to post-war fashions.*

The Medical Flapper.

The Arts Flapper.

The Science 'Flapper'.

The Slade Flapper

The Flapper's Little Sister Flapper, (who isn't anything yet.)

264.

265. *A view of the South Cloisters between the two world wars, showing along the wall the photographs of those who died in 1914-18. The South Cloisters suffered severely in the second world war (see 341.), and in Richardson's post-war reconstruction the pillars down the centre were not replaced. The* Marmor Homericum *which can be seen at the far end survived the war; it was presented by George Grote at the time when the Cloisters were glazed in 1865. An unusual creation out of pieces of marble by the Baron Triqueti, it shows various scenes from the works of Homer.*

265.

266. *The College Christmas and New Year card for 1915-16 sent jointly by the Provost and the President of the Union to all members of the College serving in the forces.*

1915

1916

· GREETINGS · AND · BEST · WISHES · FROM · UNIVERSITY · COLLEGE · LONDON ·

266.

267. An aerial photograph of the College and its vicinity taken in about 1920 before motor traffic had begun to make much impact. It shows the empty site in Gower Street cleared ready for the construction of the Anatomy building designed by Simpson himself and opened in 1923. This photograph also contains the only view known to have survived the bombing in 1940 of the Carey Foster Laboratory (see also 129.).

Between the 1890s and the 1920s, the expansion in the College's activities was matched by striking developments in the buildings. (Compare 267. with 172.) First the Front Quadrangle was closed in by the new buildings added to the North and South Wings and fronting on to Gower Street – Engineering, Architecture and Statistics. Secondly, Physics, Chemistry, Physiology, Pharmacology and Anatomy began the process whereby the larger science departments moved out of the original building into more generous quarters on the periphery, leaving the main building for the most part to the Library, administration and Arts.

After westward and northward moves up to the 1920s, further expansion was to

268.

268. A plan of the College prepared by F. M. Simpson in 1923, after his term as Professor of Architecture; it shows the distribution of departments shortly before the Centenary, but is rather inconsistent in its dating of the various buildings.

be eastward and southward (compare also with *337.*).

In 1905-07, the two distinctive round observatories were built on the lawns of the Front Quad. These additions were partly the initiative of Karl Pearson, and partly of M. T. M. Ormsby, later Professor of Municipal Engineering, whose interest was in their relevance to surveying courses as well as astronomy. The Chadwick Trustees largely paid for one, and the Drapers' Company largely for the other. They remained in use up to the second world war, serving subsequently for the storing of garden tools and the teaching of classics; the latter activity has now yielded to the manager of the College branch of the National Westminster bank.

The third stage of Starling's plans for medical sciences achieved completion with the opening of the Anatomy Building in 1923. This was funded by the Rockefeller Foundation as an expression of American friendship towards the British Empire. The £370,000 given was the College's largest benefaction. The building adjoins a further extension to the Institute of Physiology and faces the Medical School across Gower Street; all these buildings are physically linked, with the intention of encouraging the correlation of their activities, even the Medical School being connected by a tunnel under Gower Street.

In 1923 also, Anatomy was strengthened by the transfer of Histology and Embryology from Physiology; 'paradoxical as it may appear', wrote Sir Grafton Elliot Smith, Thane's successor as Professor of Anatomy, 'the reforming zeal of Professor Sharpey at this College seventy years ago had as one of its ultimate results the crippling of anatomical effort in England...' Anatomy had become very largely a descriptive science and by restoring to it the study of the nervous system from its development and growth to its degeneration, Elliott Smith laid the foundation of a tradition of research on the brain and the lower nervous system which is still producing striking experi-

mental results today. He is also remembered for his diffusionist anthropological theories on the development of culture, theories which in their extreme form led to the view that all culture was ultimately derived from Ancient Egypt. Whatever the value of his theories, Elliot Smith made UCL a centre for both physical and cultural anthropology and the current Department of Anthropology descends from his work. Another branch of study which owes its origins to the growth of Anatomy in the 1920s is the History of Medicine, still active

269. Sir Grafton Elliot Smith, FRS, Professor of Anatomy, 1919-36, working in his laboratory.

270. The Anatomy Building, hailed in the press as 'the last word in modern medical architecture' on the occasion of its opening by King George V in 1923.

as a sub-department, latterly with great support from the Wellcome Foundation.

In Physiology, Starling's successor when he gave up the Jodrell Chair was A. V. Hill, who soon after his arrival received the Nobel Prize for his work on the energy cycle associated with the contraction of muscles. He only held the Chair for three years, but remained at UCL until his retirement in 1951 as a Royal Society Research Professor. This relieved him of responsibility for teaching and he developed a very influential research unit within Physiology, which worked on problems in the physics of muscle and nerve function and which after his retirement became the Department of Biophysics. Hill was a public man, serving on many national and international bodies; he was also MP for the University of Cambridge during the war and President of the British Association in 1952. Charles Lovatt Evans succeeded Hill when he gave up the Jodrell Chair in 1926; he had for many years worked with Starling on the functioning of the heart and he continued the tradition of research in this area.

271.

272.

271. A. V Hill, CH, FRS, Jodrell Professor of Physiology, 1923-26, and Foulerton Research Professor, 1926-51, being chaired by students in 1923 outside the Institute of Physiology in celebration of his Nobel Prize; wearing the white coat is Sir Alan Parkes, FRS, as a young researcher, who virtually lived in College for eight years, producing twenty papers a year, snatching sleep in a seminar room and who was rewarded with the FRS at thirty-two.

272. The monument to Sir Charles Lovatt Evans, FRS, erected in the entrance to the Institute.

In the new Physiology building of 1909, there was already provision for 'chemical physiology', thanks to R. H. A. Plimmer, Assistant Professor and later Reader in what was a new subject. He was succeeded in 1919 by J. C. Drummond, who became the first Professor of Biochemistry in 1922; predictably enough, the new Chair was funded by the Rockefeller Foundation. The Professor of Pharmacology, A. J. Clark, with unprecedented generosity in a Head of Department, gave up some space to the new unit, and Pharmacology did not return to its 1912 boundaries until 1960, when Biochemistry moved on. Drummond's interests lay in nutrition and especially in vitamins, in the analysis, identification and even naming of which he played a notable part. He always sustained a broad range of interests, which extended later to practical questions of nutrition policy and to the history of diet on which he published *The Englishman's Food* in 1939. He was most successful in making his unit exercise an influence out of all proportion to its size. During the second world war, he became Scientific Adviser to the Ministry of Food and, after it, resigned his Chair to become Director of Research for Boots. He, his wife and their daughter were murdered while camping in France in 1952, a sensational and unsolved crime. Biochemistry was restored after the war-time chaos by Sir Frank Young, who created the independent Department in the subject. Between 1958 and 1961, it moved into its new quarters in the Biological Sciences building, by which time it was offering undergraduate as well as postgraduate courses. The developing interests of the Department were recognised in 1990 when its name was changed to 'Biochemistry and Molecular Biology'.

273. Sir Jack Drummond, FRS, Professor of Biochemistry, 1922-45.

274. Sir William Bragg, FRS, Professor of Physics, 1915-23, winner of the Nobel Prize for Physics in 1915.

275. Micaiah J. M. Hill, FRS, Professor of Mathematics, 1884-1924, Vice-Chancellor of the University of London, 1909-11, photographed at his desk for the Sphere in 1921.

276. L. N. G. Filon, FRS, Professor of Applied Mathematics, 1912-37, Vice-Chancellor of the University of London, 1933-35, photographed in the common room.

273.

A research school of physics in the sense in which it would be understood today, does not go back earlier than the twenties and owes its origin to Sir William Bragg and to his successors A. W. Porter, Professor of Physics, 1924-28, and E.N. da C. Andrade (see *387.*), Bragg graduated in Cambridge in 1884 and soon afterwards went to Australia where he held the Chair of Mathematics and Physics in Adelaide. He came back to Leeds in 1909 and moved to the Quain Chair at UCL in 1915. In the same year he received the Nobel Prize for Physics, jointly with his son, later Sir Lawrence Bragg. He had been quite unusual in starting serious research relatively late in his career. He was already in his forties when, in 1904, he began to be fascinated by the work then being done in the areas of radio-activity and X-rays. In particular, he and his son succeeded in establishing a technique for studying the arrangement of atoms in a crystal by the use of X-rays. This was basic work which helped to lay the foundations for the science of crystallography. Amongst Bragg's research students in this period at UCL was Kathleen Lonsdale, later to be Professor of Crystallography in the Department of Chemistry (see *382.*).

L. N. G. Filon was of French origin; he came to UCL as a student and became a faithful pupil of M. G. M. Hill and Karl Pearson. He became a Lecturer in Pure Mathematics in 1903, but worked on the theory of stresses and, after Pearson moved over to Eugenics, Filon succeeded him in the Chair of Applied Mathematics, which he held until 1937. He became progressively more of a figure in academic administration, acting as the first Director of the Mill Hill Observatory in 1929, becoming Vice-Chancellor of the University in 1933, and serving as Vice-President of the Royal Society in 1935-37.

One of the most prolonged research projects which the College had seen was the work pioneered by Filon together with E. G. Coker on photoelasticity between 1909 and 1934 and the resumed programme of research undertaken by their successors after the war. In 1909 Coker was head of the Engineering Department at Finsbury Technical College and Filon still a lecturer in Pure Mathematics at UCL. Filon had worked on elasticity in connection with the bending of beams and he was much impressed by a paper of which Coker was joint author which suggested that the use of xylonite models would allow the stresses in engineering components to be studied by optical techniques. Filon supplied the theory, Coker the practical application. In 1912 Filon, as Professor of Applied Mathematics, obtained his own laboratory; two years later, Coker became a Professor at UCL, Head of the Department of Civil and Mechanical Engineering for twenty years, so that he too set up a photoelastic laboratory, which worked in parallel – sometimes uneasily – with Filon's.

Their joint publication *Treatise on Photo-elasticity* (1931) was the most authoritative account of the subject possible at that date. Coker, however, failed to convince industry of the viability of his new methods and when he retired in 1934 his laboratory was virtually abandoned and, on the outbreak of war, completely dismantled. After the war, new advances in the technique made in the USA, together with a new interest in British industry, caused the programme to be resumed; Coker's laboratory was reconstructed, and a new research group created under H. J. Jessop.

277.

278.

277. E. G. Coker, FRS, Professor of Civil and Mechanical Engineering, 1914-34, photographed with his photoelasticity students in 1919.

278. Coker's original photoelastic bench.

279. Excavation in progress in 1921 for the Hydraulics Laboratory built alongside the Engineering building underneath part of the Front Quad.

280. The assembled staff and students of Engineering, a separate Faculty since 1908, photographed during the first world war, amongst them a number of the College's most distinguished scientists who then provided teaching for Engineering students; they include Sir William Ramsay, Sir William Bragg and Karl Pearson.

280.

Two fundamental changes affected the Faculty of Arts in the years after incorporation into the University: the rise of the 'honours' degree, which enabled the students to specialise, and the proper funding of salaries, which enabled the professors to become full-time. The teaching of history especially was revolutionised. From 1896 the honours degree in the subject was available, and from 1905 the 'internal' honours degree in the re-organised University. The moving spirit in the ensuing transformation was not F. C. Montague, Beesly's successor in the Chair of History, 1893-1927, 'a tolerant rationalist and a blameless epicurean', but the redoubtable Tudor historian A. F. Pollard. In 1903 there was a vacancy in the Chair of Constitutional Law and History and the two outstanding candidates were Pollard and W. S. (later Sir William) Holdsworth. The appointing committee hit on the idea of splitting the Chair into two and taking them both: 'why not?', suggested the presiding genius; 'there is no stipend for either, and it will cost the College no more to have two chairs than one'.

Pollard had worked in the 1890s as Assistant Editor of the *Dictionary of National Biography*, and involvement in that great exercise in scholarly co-operative

282.

organisation proved formative. It provided the model for his postgraduate seminar and the germ of the Institute of Historical Research which he founded in 1920. He was also the architect of two other major developments in the subject: he created the School of History, still the only major example of co-operation in teaching between the various colleges of the University of London, and, at a meeting at UCL in 1906, he founded the Historical Association as a forum for the teachers of the expanding subject. Ten years later, Pollard became first editor of its journal, *History*. Since 1950, two years after his death, Pollard has been commemorated, in a way that would have shocked him, in the *Pollardian*, the irreverent journal of the History students.

The study of German was placed on a firm academic footing by Robert Priebsch, the correct but kind Austrian who held the Chair of German for thirty-three years from 1898. Priebsch was a medievalist with a consuming passion for manuscripts; his great published work was a catalogue of German manuscripts in England. In building up a notable Department of German, Priebsch was considerably aided by John G. Robertson, a modernist, who between 1903 and 1933 held a chair of German shared with Bedford College, and who also succeeded W. P. Ker as Director of Scandinavian Studies.

281. A. F. Pollard, FBA, Professor of Constitutional History, 1903-07, of English History, 1907-27, and then, while Director of the Institute of Historical Research, again of Constitutional History, 1927-31.

282. Robert Priebsch, Professor of German Language and Literature, 1889-1931, in the photograph he presented to his seminar after his retirement.

281.

A conspicuous figure in Anglo-Italian life was Antonio Cippico, a writer and journalist who became a teacher of Italian before the first world war and Professor of Italian in 1918. A fervent and poetic Italian patriot, he was one of the earliest apostles of the Fascist movement and founder of the Fascio of London, becoming a senator after Mussolini's march on Rome in 1922. For a few years he combined his public duties in Rome with his teaching in London, but resigned in 1925 to become Italian delegate to the League of Nations.

Most of the teachers of Law, if distinguished, were transient figures following their professional careers. One traditional figure who stayed for 42 years was A. F. Murison, Professor of Roman Law from 1884 to 1925. A Scottish schoolmaster turned barrister, he set himself the enormous task of collating the codices of the text of the *Institutes* of Justinian distributed all over the libraries of Europe. He mastered every European language, except only Turkish, but never finished his undertaking; his voluminous transcripts and notes remain in the Library, untouched since his death in 1934. Murison was obliged to support himself by vast quantities of miscellaneous lecturing, examining, translating and journalism. For the first thirty years of the

283.

tenure of his Chair he claimed he was paid no more that £30 per annum. Only after 1912 was the old system phased out by which the unendowed professors were paid 5s. in the guinea out of the students' fees. H. F. Jolowicz, Murison's successor in 1931, was guaranteed £800 per annum. This trend was to have profound effects on the nature and structure of academic life.

284.

283. A. F. Murison, Professor of Roman Law, 1884-1925, and of Jurisprudence, 1901-25, photographed as Dean of the Faculty of Law in 1921.

284. Antonio Cippico, Professor of Italian, 1918-25, as shown on the medal established in his honour, itself a fine period-piece.

The great age of rags spanned the period between the two world wars. It began before 1914, as can be seen from the jollifications on Ladysmith night in 1900 involving the capture of Phineas (see *223.-227.*). In the heyday of rags there were some great set-piece battles with King's, the target being Reggie, their lion mascot, the weapons including flour, sprays of water, mud, deception, furniture vans and debagging. Annual bonfires were a great institution too, until the Provost announced in 1952 that 'much to his regret he cannot sanction a bonfire in the Main Quadrangle this year'. The era of indulging in such escapades had begun to fade, and the original pressing need to raise money in this way had passed.

285.

286.

285-287. Scenes from the great age of rags.

288. Phineas, the College's great symbol on such occasions, being borne triumphantly out of the front gates in 1932.

288.

159

289. The Front Quad in November
1927 during one of the greatest of
the battles against the students of
King's College.

289.

The Centenary of the College was celebrated in some style in June 1927. It was inaugurated by the visit of King George V and Queen Mary, and included – inevitably – a new Appeal for funds, as well as the opening of the Great Hall, the receiving of delegates from universities throughout the world, a series of lectures, a variety of exhibitions and dinners, and a service of thanksgiving in Westminster Abbey. The Students' Union quite reasonably objected to the sectarian nature of this last celebration, but the Centenary as a whole was found an agreeable exercise in self-congratulation. The King made an interesting and uncharacteristically controversial point in his speech, one which the press reported as producing cheers of an enthusiasm that broke royal protocol. 'The State', he said, 'now aids University Institutions on a scale which, to your founders, would have seemed impossible, but there are limits to public assistance. Moreover there is some danger to our national ideas of University freedom in too great reliance upon State grants.'

G. K. Chesterton, a former student, was in more characteristic mood for his lecture a few days later. 'It was at the Slade School', he claimed, 'that I discovered that I should never be an artist; it was at the lectures of Professor A. E. Housman that I discovered that I should never be a scholar; and it was at the lectures of Professor W. P. Ker that I discovered that I should never be a literary man. The warning, alas! fell on heedless ears, and I still attempted the practice of writing, which, let me tell you in the name of the whole Slade School, is very much easier than the practice of drawing and painting'. He went on, with perhaps a touch of exaggeration, to claim that the Centenary was in fact that of the opening of the modern world.

290.

291.

290. The cover of the Rag Magazine produced on the occasion of the celebration of the College's Centenary in 1927.

291. Some undergraduettes flourishing the Centenary Rag Magazine for sale.

292. King George V and Queen Mary in procession through the Front Quad after their official visit to the College in June 1927.

292.

293.

294.

293&294. The King and Queen descending the Portico steps and processing to tea on the Front Lawn on the occasion of their Centenary visit.

295. The King and Queen with Sir Gregory Foster, the Provost, Sir William Beveridge, Director of the LSE and Vice-Chancellor of the University of London at the time, and Lord Chelmsford, Chairman of the College Committee, 1922-32. The royal party went on to visit the exhibition in the Slade, where the King expressed his distaste for Cubism to Tonks, who was able to assure him he would 'find none here'.

296. The 208 delegates from other universities being photographed on the steps of the Portico.

296.

299.

297.

298.

300.

297. H. Hale Bellot, author of the definitive Centenary history of the College, first Commonwealth Fund Professor of American History, 1930-55, and Vice-Chancellor of the University of London, 1951-53.

298. Another well-remembered historian: Norman H. Baynes, FBA, Dean of the Faculty of Arts at the time of the Centenary, Professor of Byzantine History, 1931-42.

299. Hanslip Fletcher's drawing of the Great Hall as designed by Richardson.

300. The dedication of the new Great Hall by Prince Arthur of Connaught in June 1927 as a memorial to the dead of the first world war. It was entirely destroyed in the second.

301.

301. The Gustave Tuck Theatre as it then was, before destruction in the second world war.

302.

The College had never had a Great Hall since the abandoning of the one originally planned by Wilkins and it was decided to remedy this by a suitable conversion of All Saints' Church built by Donaldson in 1846 at the rear of the College. The building was in a dilapidated state when the College bought it in 1914. After the war it was agreed that it should also serve as a war memorial to the 301 members of the College who had been killed. The reconstruction was finely undertaken by A.E. Richardson, the Professor of Architecture, and the opening constituted a major part of the Centenary celebrations. The Appeal was less successful. The aim was to raise £500,000 but such was the difficulty in deciding how it should be spent that the centenary had to be postponed from February 1926 to June 1927. Then, as it turned out, the time chosen was one of deepening economic depression, and by July 1930 less than half the expected total had been raised, and the Appeal was closed.

One success resulting from the appeal was the benefaction of Gustave Tuck, Treasurer and President of the Jewish Historical Society, for the rebuilding of the Mocatta Library and the provision of a new lecture theatre. Much of the Mocatta collection was destroyed in the second world war, but the renewed library is now once again an important resource for the activities of the Department of Hebrew and Jewish Studies. In the week of the Centenary celebrations, it was finally settled that the University of London should acquire a central headquarters site, to the south of UCL, after its years in Burlington House and in South Kensington. After complicated negotiations involving the Duke of Bedford and the government, Beveridge and the Rockefeller Foundation, the scene was set for Senate House to rear its head in Bloomsbury.

303.

302. The Exhibition Gallery being opened by Lord and Lady Duveen in 1930, with Professor Sir John Rose Bradford, FRS, Chairman of the College Committee, 1932-35, in attendance, and some of the Rembrandt etchings in the background. In 1981, after being used for other purposes since the war, the room was re-opened as the Strang Print Room.

303. The bronze plaque erected in the Library to Gustave Tuck in 1932.

304.

The enormous popularity of Sir Gregory Foster as Provost was shown by the tumultuous reception he was given in February 1926 on his return from a year's leave of absence spent in South Africa. Charabancs full of students provided an exuberant escort from his home to 'the largest number of students and staff ever gathered' in the Front Quad. There was much shouting of what had become – and was for some years to remain – the College chant:

Foster, Foster, Gregory Foster,
Gower Street, Gower Street, UCL.

While he had been away, his duties had been carried out by a triumvirate of Pro-Provosts: Seton, the Secretary; H. E. Butler, the Professor of Latin; and Col. H. J. Harris, the Senior Tutor – known collectively as the world, the flesh and the devil. Less than a year later, on the eve of the Centenary celebrations which he had done much to plan, Seton died suddenly. He was succeeded by C. O. G. Douie, an extremely able administrator from the Ministry of Education and a civilised man of wide interests and tastes. At the end of 1929, Foster retired as Provost to concentrate on being Vice-Chancellor of the University under its new statutes. The second Provost was Sir Allen Mawer, a former graduate student of the College who had gone on to become Professor of English at Newcastle and then at Liverpool. His great passion was English place names, and he did more than anyone to put their study on a rigorous basis.

305.

304. Sir Allen Mawer, FBA, Foster's successor as Provost, 1930-42.

305. The scene in the Front Quad as Sir Gregory Foster was welcomed back in 1926 after his year's leave.

306. C. O. G. Douie, Secretary of the College, 1927-38, as painted by Elizabeth Polunin of the Slade.

306.

307. The pre-war Ramsay Memorial Laboratory of Chemical Engineering.

308. The formal opening of the Ramsay Memorial Laboratory by the Duke of Kent in 1931; on his left W. E. Gibbs, the second Professor, 1928-34, and on his right Lord Chelmsford.

The he major innovation in the Faculty of Engineering between the wars was the creation of the Department of Chemical Engineering in 1923. The first Professor of the subject in the country was E. C. Williams, who after putting the Department on its feet became Research Director for Shell in California. Both the new Chair and the laboratories which followed were a memorial to Sir William Ramsay, who had died in 1916. Half the money raised by the Memorial Fund was put towards the new Department, which also received substantial support from industry. The first temporary accommodation was opened in 1924 in the old St Pancras Vestry Hall, while next door the site of 21 and 23 Gordon Street was being used for the building of completely new laboratories, designed by A.E. Richardson, the first of many College buildings for which he was to be responsible. Postgraduate courses started from the beginning with a good deal of improvisation; the undergraduate degree dates from 1938. The new laboratories, opened in 1931, suffered severe bomb-damage in the war.

309. The retirement gathering for E. J. Garwood, FRS, Professor of Geology, 1901-31, the architect of the modern Geology Department; many of his pupils over the thirty years are to be seen, including Marie Stopes.

169

310.

310. The new quarters for the Department of Zoology created out of the former Shoolbreds' warehouse and mattress factory – part of the addition to the College named Foster Court in honour of Sir Gregory Foster who died just before they were acquired in 1931.

311. The Earl of Athlone, as Chancellor of the University, on his way to open Foster Court in June 1933, seen through the Physiology Arch.

312. The Senior Laboratory in the new Department of Zoology.

311.

Further expansion of the College buildings was made possible by the bankruptcy in the depression of the early 1930s of Shoolbreds, a once-famous department store in Tottenham Court Road. Their workshops and stables lay immediately to the south of the College site, and D.M.S. Watson decided that suitably converted they could contain adequate premises for the Department of Zoology and Comparative Anatomy which was outgrowing the quarters created for Lankester in the North Wing (see p. 89). Since succeeding to

312.

the Jodrell Chair in 1921, Watson had nurtured plans for a Zoology expansion parallel to Elliot Smith's development of human biology in the enlarged Department of Anatomy. The Rockefeller Foundation provided another endowment for this purpose. The acquisition of Shoolbred's Mews in 1931 was a good deal more than half financed by the advance sale of rather less than a third of the buildings to the National Central Library, then being established with Carnegie money; in this skilful manoeuvre the College's well-placed Highland connections were deftly deployed, as was, apparently, the necessary Talisker whisky over lunch. The rest of the utilitarian buildings, erected by Shoolbreds in the 1890s, were straightforwardly reconstructed as laboratories and teaching rooms by A. E. Richardson. Watson continued his important contributions to zoology and palaeontology until his retirement from the Jodrell Chair in 1951, and afterwards as an Honorary Research Associate until 1965, when his resignation ended fifty-three years of continuous service to the College. When the National Central Library building was re-acquired by the College in 1967, mainly for use as an annexe to the Library, it was renamed the 'D. M. S. Watson Library'. Both this and the western part of the Foster Court buildings housing the Departments of Geography, English, Scandinavian Studies and Egyptology (the latter in the former

313. The oldest architectural feature of the College site, the Pewterers' Gate, dated 1668, and believed to have been designed by Sir Christopher Wren. It was removed from its original position at Pewterers' Hall in the City to its present site at the rear of what is now the Medawar Building in 1932 by Sir Albert Richardson as one of the several 'follies' among the College buildings for which he was responsible. Another curiosity of Richardson's, smaller but equally striking, is the 'Adam and Eve' door-handles of the Medawar building.

stables) were long overdue for replacement. Plans were drawn up by Anthony Cox in 1972 for a major redevelopment involving a large new School of Medicine as proposed by a Royal Commission chaired by Lord Todd in 1968. Much thought was given to these proposals in the 1970s, but eventually the government withdrew its funding. The subsequent building developments took place elsewhere, and the problems of the Foster Court buildings and what is now called the 'Bloomsbury Science Library' remain.

314. J. P. Hill, FRS, Jodrell Professor of Zoology, 1906-21, and subsequently the pioneering Professor of Embryology, 1921-38.

315. D. M. S. Watson, FRS, Jodrell Professor of Zoology, 1921-51.

318.

316.

316&317. Two cartoons in the
possession of the Department of
Psychology, one showing S. J. F.
Philpott, a member of the staff of
the Department from 1920 until
1952, together with Professor
Spearman and J. T. Raper, the
Department's indispensable
Technical Assistant, in pursuit of
'general intelligence', the origins of
the concept of 'IQ', the other shows
J. C. Flugel on the same quest.

317.

In the earliest years of the College, John
Conolly and John Elliotson as professors
of medicine had taken an interest in
psychological problems (see pp. 33, 55), but
the origins of a more systematic approach
to the subject are to be found in the
Department of Philosophy in the 1890s.
James Sully, who succeeded Croom Robertson as Grote Professor was more of a
psychologist than a philosopher. He was a
prime mover in the creation of the British
Psychological Society, founded at UCL in
1902. A laboratory for experimental psychology was established in 1897. Housed
originally in a small room that doubled as a
library store, it was the first such laboratory
in England which in this respect lagged
behind Germany and the United States. It
was equipped with apparatus brought from
Freiburg, and put under the charge of W. H.
Rivers, though he left after a year to take
part in the famous Cambridge anthropological expedition to Torres Straits.

In 1903 William McDougall was made
Reader in Experimental Psychology, but
significant work in the new subject really
began in 1907 with his successor, the
German-trained Charles Spearman, and
with the move to more spacious quarters in
the South Wing. Spearman became Grote
Professor in 1911, and later, in 1928, the
Chair of Psychology was established for
him. One of his earliest interests was in the
concept of 'general intelligence' or 'G' and
in ways of measuring it through the
application to psychological problems of

319.

the techniques of correlation developed by Galton and Pearson (see p. 105). J. C. Flugel joined Spearman as his Assistant in 1909, and remained a member of the Department for virtually the whole of the rest of his life. He resigned as Assistant Professor of Psychology in 1943, finding life in war-time Aberystwyth intolerable, but became a

Special Lecturer on the Department's return to London after the war until his death ten years later in 1955. For many years he gave pioneering lectures on Freudian psycho-analysis, and wrote an interesting book on *The Psychology of Clothes*.

The lines of research opened up by Spearman were developed by his successor, Sir Cyril Burt. In 1943 he had been appointed by the LCC to be the first official psychologist to an educational authority, and in 1924 became Professor of Education at the Institute of Education. He conducted classic research on delinquent and mal-adjusted children, research which involved his becoming for a time a member of a criminal gang who accepted him as 'Charlie the parson'. His work on intelligence testing was one of the influences on the organisa-tion of secondary education after the 1944 Act. Burt's thesis that differences in intelli-gence are to a considerable extent genetic has become the focus of much controversy since his death in 1971, and he came to be accused in the press of inventing not only some of his data, but also mythical female collaborators; these unproven charges were rejected by his many admirers.

320. Experiments in progress in the Psychology Laboratory in the South Wing c. 1930.

320.

321. Daniel Jones, creator of a new Department as Professor of Phonetics, 1921-49.

'antəni. 'frɛndz, 'roumənz, 'kʌntrimɛn, 'lɛnd mi: jɔːr 'iəz;
ai 'kʌm tu 'bɛri *'siːzə, 'nɔt tu 'preiz him.
ði 'iːvil ðət mɛn 'du: 'livz 'ɑːftə ðɛm;
ðə 'gud iz 'ɔft in'təːrid wið ðɛə 'bounz;

'antəni. 'frɛndz, 'roːmənz, 'kʏntrimɛn, 'lɛnd mi: juːɹ 'iːɹz;
əi 'kʏm tu 'bɛri 'seːzəɹ, 'nɔt tu 'prɛːz hiṁ.
ði 'iːvil ðat mɛn 'du: 'livz 'aftəɹ ðɛm;
ðə 'gud iz 'ɔft in'taːrid wið ðɛːɹ 'boːnz;

ωʃ [ɜω, ωʃ૦ ੭ʃŒ ૦ʃ ωʃɜω]૦૦Iℽ ωʃɜ.
ωʃ ੭ʃ૦ ʃω ƒ੭૦ ſω·૦ʃω·ʃ૦ ੭ʃω ωʃℽ ੭ƒ૦ω.

322. Three transcriptions of Anthony's speech from Julius Caesar: the first two are by Jones and are in modern and Elizabethan pronunciation respectively; the third is in Alexander Melville Bell's 'visible speech'.

323. Work in progress in the Phonetics Laboratory, c. 1930, with the Lioretgraph, a device which obtained oscillograms of speech from a gramophone record.

The study of phonetics might be said to go back to the work of Alexander Melville Bell, who lectured on speech at the College between 1866 and 1870 and who devised a phonetic script which he called 'visible speech'; he was assisted by his son Alexander Graham Bell, then a student at the College and later the inventor of the telephone. It was not, however, until 1907 that systematic teaching began with the appointment of Daniel Jones. At first the courses were under the auspices of the English and modern languages departments and were mainly offered to those who were intending to become language teachers. Jones worked alone for ten years, but by 1918 the subject had expanded to include more and more languages and also the historical aspects of phonetics; experimental phonetics too had obtained a toe-hold with the creation of a small laboratory in 1911. With encouragement from Gregory Foster, the subject expanded rapidly after the war and by 1921 Jones had become the first Professor of the subject and there were nine full-time assistants. In 1922 the Department moved to the Gordon Square premises which it has occupied ever since. By the time Daniel Jones retired in 1949, he had created a thriving Department with a world-wide reputation.

174

Director of Scandinavian Studies and was an active secretary of the Communications Research Centre in its early days, fostering two areas which grew into independent departments in the course of the sixties. It was also in his Department that Medieval Archaeology started with the appointment of D. M. Wilson, now Director of the British Museum; the subject later moved into Scandinavian Studies and then into History, and has now moved on to the Institute of Archaeology. But above all Smith was the man who kept the Place Names Survey moving, so that it remained a very vigorous element in UCL.

The Department now includes Linguistics as well as Phonetics. The first step came in 1953 when the Communications Research Centre was set up as an experiment in interdisciplinary studies, to involve linguists, biologists and all interested in any form of communication both verbal and non-verbal. The enterprise was years ahead of its time, anticipating developments to be hailed in other universities as new and exciting a decade later. Its weakness was perhaps that it included too much and when M. A. K. Halliday was appointed Director in 1963, he recommended narrowing the range to human communication. In 1965 the Department of Linguistics was created, including the Centre. Six years later, it was merged with Phonetics.

Allen Mawer's main academic work, which he sustained after becoming Provost, was the methodical survey of English place-names. His initial interest came from his work on the Scandinavian influence on early England; from the inception of the English Place Names Society, which he inspired, he acted as its Director and was General Editor of its county by county survey. At UCL he found an energetic assistant in A. H. Smith, who came to the Department of English in 1930 and worked as one of its most devoted members for thirty-seven years, becoming Quain Professor of English in 1949. He also acted as

324-326. Three cartoons illustrating characteristic activities of A. H. Smith, Professor of English, 1949-67: meeting a place name with Sir Allen Mawer; travelling in style to his home at Alderton, near Tewkesbury, and at the Pierian spring.

175

327. A cartoon of Mawer as Provost with R. W. Chambers and C. J. Sisson, Professors of English, triumphing over the problems of the 1930s, from the University College Magazine *in 1934.*

328. A student demonstration in 1933 revealing other political problems of the time.

327.

328.

329.

329. Hugh Gaitskell, later Leader of the Labour Party, who taught economics at the College between 1928 and 1939, photographed in the senior common room in conversation with C. O. G. Douie.

330. The Exhibition Room (see 302.) in use as the staff dining room in the late 1930s.

330.

National and international politics began to intrude significantly into student life from the late 1920s. In 1932, the first student political society, the Socialist Society, won recognition after a battle with the College authorities. One member of the staff with strong political interests was Hugh Gaitskell, who came as an Assistant in Political Economy in 1928 and rose to be Reader and acting Head of the Department, as well as Tutor to the Higher Civil Service Students. He attended the *Tots and Quots*, a dining club, which met in Soho for scientific argument, founded by G. P. (Gip) Wells, later Professor of Zoology. In 1945 Gaitskell was offered the Chair of Political Economy, but he declined in order to stand for Parliament, becoming Chancellor of the Exchequer, 1950-51, and subsequently leader of the Labour Party until his premature death in 1963.

The College tradition of producing the cycle of 'Little Plays of St. Francis' written by Laurence Housman, the brother of A. E. Housman, began in 1925 at the suggestion of Walter Seton. They became an annual event for the Dramatic Society until 1950. Housman himself was closely involved and granted the College the right to produce the plays free of royalty. In 1937 a performance was televised, and the Dramatic Society became the first amateur group to appear on television.

331.

333.

334.

335.

332.

331. A. J. L. Cahill, Registrar of the College between 1954 and 1979, acting in one of the series of 'Little Plays of St Francis', together with their author, Laurence Housman.

332. A Slade Dance decoration of 1930 portraying Tonks, who retired in that year, and Randolph Schwabe, his successor as Slade Professor, 1930-48.

333. Three men who made their mark through their devotion to generations of students at the College: J. W. Jeaffreson, an inspiring teacher of French between 1919 and 1949.

334. H. J. Harris, second President of the Union in 1894, a teacher of mathematics until 1933, Senior Tutor, and Colonel of the University OTC.

335. N. Eumorfopoulos, a leading College figure while Demonstrator and Research Assistant in Physics from 1894 to 1942, for the last twenty-two years in an honorary capacity.

177

J. B. S. Haldane, who took his forenames from John Burdon Sanderson, his great-uncle (see p. 86), came to UCL as Professor of Genetics in 1933 and became the first Weldon Professor of Biometrics in 1937. He had made his name by a series of papers showing mathematically how Darwin's theory would actually work in terms of Mendelian genetics. He was regarded by many as a near-genius. He was also famous as one of the great popularisers of science, and moreover he had already shown his splendid patrician pugnacity against all forms of imposed authority. Throughout the thirties his politics moved leftwards; he began a remarkable series of scientific articles in the *Daily Worker*, though he did not actually join the Communist Party until 1942. His highest public fame came over the Lysenko controversy, when he stubbornly defended the Party's line, despite private misgivings both about Lysenko's theories and the Stalinist regime's exploitation of them.

His achievement as scientific theoretician was formidable, but his achievement as professor at UCL was limited by his own perversity. Cantankerous to a degree, he became a legend for mismanaging business, terrorising secretaries and abusing administrators. In 1958, he made an improbable, though in the event successful, move to India. The departure was vintage Haldane, complete with bogus political motive (revulsion at the Suez adventure, though he had already decided to go), with allegations of bad faith by the College (promises made to him about the development of his Department had, he claimed, never been fulfilled) and a silly little scandal (his second wife, Helen Spurway, once a student, later a lecturer in the Department, insisted on going to prison after an incident outside the Marlborough Arms in which she trod on a police dog's tail). Haldane's stature as a scholar survives all the aberrations; the College honours his memory through the eponymous Common Room.

336. The Claude Rogers portrait of J. B. S. Haldane, FRS, which hangs in Haldane Room.

337. A plan showing the pre-war expansion of the College into most of the 'rectangle' bounded by Gower Street, Torrington Place, Gordon Street and Gower Place.

The second world war did more damage to UCL than to any other British university or college. In September 1940 a bomb hit the buildings, entirely destroying the Great Hall and the Carey Foster Physics Laboratory. The Gustave Tuck and the Applied Mathematics Theatres were gutted, as was the Library north of the Dome. Serious damage was also done to other parts of the building. In April 1941 another air-raid led to considerable destruction by fire of the main building south of the Dome, and of the Dome itself.

The academic work of the College had already been dispersed. The crisis of 1938 had led to arrangements being made for evacuation, and in 1939 new entrants were refused and the departments immediately scattered to Aberystwyth, Bangor, Cardiff, Swansea, Sheffield, Southampton, Oxford, Cambridge and Rothamsted. The Faculty of Medical Sciences was subsequently re-united at Leatherhead, and an administrative headquarters was formed at Stansted Bury, near Ware, in Hertfordshire. The much reduced College continued in this extraor-

338. One of the series of elegant views of the College buildings drawn by J. D. M. Harvey in the years after the first world war.

338.

180

dinarily far-flung way for the duration of the war. The decision to clear the College buildings was not taken without opposition: J. B. S. Haldane was in his element when he refused to budge, continuing his work for a time, 'subject', as he reported gleefully, 'to a certain amount of siege by the College authorities'.

The Library suffered most drastically from the air-raids. The manuscripts and rare books were evacuated to the solid rock cellars of the National Library of Wales at Aberystwyth, but some 100,000 books and pamphlets were destroyed as a result of the 1940 attack. The heaviest losses were to the Science Library, the English, German, Scandinavian and Phonetics collections, and the Mocatta Library. John Wilks, the Librarian from 1926 to 1954 had been a pupil of Robert Priebsch, the Professor of German (see p. 156), himself a noted bibliophile; they had built up the best working library of German scholarship outside the German-speaking countries. It was ironic that this was one of the collections largely destroyed.

339. A photograph taken during the second world war, from virtually the same point: showing the burnt Dome across the ruins of the Carey Foster Laboratory, it reveals the extent of the damage caused by the bombings of 1940 and 1941.

339.

340. The war-time scene looking north from the Department of Pharmacology showing the extent of the destruction to the Mathematics Department, the Provost's office and the Council Room.

341. The site of the Great Hall and the Carey Foster Physics Laboratory after the bombing of September 1940.

342. The gutted South Cloisters in April 1941.

343.

343. The roof of the Library north
of the Dome as it appeared in
September 1940.

344. The interior of the Science
library at the same date, revealing
the massive extent of the damage
sustained.

344.

345.

346.

345.&346. Books from the Library being dried out and inspected after the air-raid.

347. The ruins of the Ramsay Memorial Laboratory of Chemical Engineering in 1941, with (in military uniform) M. B. Donald, later to be Professor of Chemical Engineering, 1951-65.

The difficulties of life for the remaining students and staff in the dispersed elements of the College were considerable. In Physics, for example, sent to the University College of North Wales at Bangor, there were various demarcation disputes with the host department. It became necessary for Orson Wood, the Tutor to Science Students, to improvise a laboratory in a converted bicycle shop in the High Street, blocking up the windows so that students could work unobserved by passers-by. Soon after the Faculty of Engineering moved to Swansea the students claimed that their lodgings were disturbed by so many air-raids that they might as well move back to less makeshift accommodation in London.

In Oxford, the Slade was amalgamated with the Ruskin Drawing School under the joint direction of Randolph Schwabe as Slade Professor and Albert Rutherston, the Ruskin Master of Drawing, himself, like his brother, Sir William Rothenstein, a former Slade student. The Slade students were considered to have contributed much to the gaiety of Oxford during the grim war years. Towards the end of the war, all the main College deeds were flooded in the place of safety to which they had been taken at Stansted Bury; an unreadable solid mass, the are still preserved in the College safe until the papyrologists have time to apply the latest techniques of restoration. Many other records were destroyed at the time of the bombing of the College.

R. W. Chambers (see p. 138) went to give brilliantly allusive lectures on the history of the College to the students in exile in Aberystwyth and Bangor, but collapsed on the way to deliver another in Swansea: he died, it was said, of a broken heart following the destruction of so much of the Library he had created and of the College he had loved. Sir Allen Mawer died a few weeks later in 1942 on his way from Stansted Bury to a committee meeting in London. He had suffered from the strain of much travelling in his efforts to hold the scattered fragments of the College together.

348.

348. Stansted Bury, the war-time home of the College administration and of the Library.

349. The improvised Physics Laboratory of 1942 in an old bicycle shop in Bangor High Street.

350. The evacuated staff of UCL, mainly the Faculty of Arts, at Bangor.

351. Students and staff of the Department of Chemistry in evacuation at Aberystwyth.

349.

Dr D. R. (later Sir David) Pye became Provost of a deserted and ruinous College in 1943 in which 'there was hardly a square foot of glass'. He was an engineer with a considerable academic and administrative reputation. In Cambridge, he had done pioneer work on the internal combustion engine and, as Director of Scientific Research for the Air Ministry, on the development of jet propulsion. He nursed the College through its extremely difficult move back to the blitzed buildings and the planning of the post-war rebuilding. 'Refectory accommodation in 1939 was totally inadequate', propounded the first plan for reconstruction produced in June 1943, 'Common Rooms were equally so and were inconveniently scattered. It is regarded as an essential feature of the replanned College that the amenity accommodation shall be conveniently grouped round a central position...' The confident hopes of 1943 were never to be realised in the post-war world.

352.

Pye, Pi *and pie in the sky.*

352. A model of the redevelopment of the College site hoped for in the early 1950s.

353. Sir David Pye, FRS, the third Provost, 1943-51.

354. The first issue of the students' newspaper Pi, *named in Pye's honour, in 1946.*

353.

Thursday February 21st, 1946.
Number 1.   **Price 2d.**

Next Month UCL Will Be
119 YEARS OLD

Societies Provide
Large-Scale Entertainment

PREPARATIONS for Foundation Week, which begins Monday, March 11th and continues until the 18th, are well advanced. A series of activities is planned which will extend over a fortnight. These activities will include a concert, two pre-Foundation Week plays, soccer and rugger matches, a debate, the Foundation Ball, and numerous dinners, parties and hops. The Foundation speaker this year will be the Very Reverend the Lord Bishop Barnes of Birmingham.

The festivities will begin as the Dramatic Society gives five performances of a double bill of two plays, between Wednesday, March 6th and March 8th. One of the plays is to be "Cain," produced by Christopher Beedell, and "The Lying Valet," produced by Alan Barlow. In spite of attacks of 'flu among the cast, rehearsals and stagework are progressing satisfactorily in the gymnasium. The Saturday matinee performance of the plays is to be given in aid of the Q-Camps for maladjusted children.

Success To New College Newspaper

—the Provost

In a College the size of ours communications are a difficult problem. University College is unique in the number and variety of Faculties and Departments within its walls. In no other College can Chemists and Physicists rub shoulders with the Fine Arts, or Engineers learn something of the ways of Lawyers, Phoneticians, and Medicos. But to make the most of our opportunities we need to have a sense of corporate membership, which means, in effect, that the doings of each Department should be a matter of interest to all. There are passengers in every community who contribute little and look to others to provide for them ; but often they are passengers because nothing has yet awakened an interest in their surroundings which is latent nevertheless ; and so it must be in the College.

A Newspaper specially adapted to the needs and interests of Students, post-graduate as well as under-graduate, can be an ideal medium through which to promote a sense of corporate interest which embraces all the varied activities in the College. For this reason I welcome most warmly the appearance of my namesake.

I am told by the Editorial Committee that no one of their number is willing to accept responsibility for having suggested the name of their baby ; but that having been collectively evolved, the more it was queried, frowned upon, laughed out of Court, the more impossible it was either to neglect or to forget it. If the contents of Pi have the qualities of its name, success will be assured and Pi will extend as the mathematicians would have us believe, to an infinite series of numbers.

Dramatic Society's work ends as Foundation Week begins, and all connected with the plays hope to relax.

On Tuesday, March 12th, the Foundation Concert will be held in Friend's House. The 90-minute programme, starting at 6.30 p.m., will include Schubert's Sixth Symphony and performances by the Music Society Choir of Handel's "Acis and Galatea " and the " Danse Polotusienne," from Borodin's " Prince Igor."

University College teams take the field on Wednesday, March 13th, to play against King's. Phineas will be present. The matches to be played will include Soccer, Rugger, Men's and Women's hockey matches, Lacrosse and Netball. University College teams are determined to gain victories and avenge the defeats suffered during King's Commemoration Week. As a friendly gesture, however, King's teams may be invited to a Hop in the Gym. on the night of the game.

The Debating Society takes over on Friday, the 15th, during their Foundation Debate, which is to be held in the U.C.L. Gymnasium. Dr. Mathieux, Dean of St. Paul's, is among the speakers invited to hold forth on the motion " That the world is peopled by wicked sharps and good flats." There will be a Debates' Dinner afterwards.

Continued on page 4, column 1

EXAMINATIONS PREVENT MEDICS JOINING FUN

MR. M. GREENBERG, a student of the Faculty of Medical Sciences, announced at a recent unofficial meeting that seventy medical students would be unable to participate in the Foundation Ball, owing to 2nd M.B. examinations commencing on March 18th. In a letter from the Medical Society to the Secretary of the I.U.S.C., it was suggested that the Ball should be held one week earlier, as this arrangement would be acceptable to most medical students, who would not mind spending a few of their pre-examination hours relaxing at the dance.

It appears that no compromise was possible, as it is extremely difficult to book a hall suitable for a U.C.L. function of this type and it was impossible to alter the date of the arranged booking.

When the date for Foundation Week was announced at a Union Society meeting held on December 8th, no serious protest was raised by the Medical member present, and therefore arrangements proceeded. An official recording has been made in the Inter Union Standing Committee's minutes to prevent recurrence of this unfortunate situation. Meanwhile, seventy medical students will not be present at the Foundation Ball. A further 60 Junior 2nd M.B. Students will be unable to attend since they go down on the 16th to make room for the senior examinations.

RECONSTRUCTION DELAYED BY HOUSING PROGRAMME

PLANS for the rebuilding of University College, prepared by Professor Richardson, of Architecture, are now well advanced. This opportunity for replanning the College in a style worthy of its needs and traditions has been provided by the otherwise disastrous destruction of many buildings by high-explosive and incendiary bombs. Unfortunately, this important work has been temporarily suspended, as the critical housing situation has precluded the issue of the necessary permits for buildings other than dwellings.

In the office of Mr. Taylor, the Superintendent of Works, there is a large file of carefully drawn plans. But until the Ministry of Works issues a permit, and contracts are drawn up, no start can be made on the rehabilitation of the Main Building or the excavation of ground to the East of it for new quadrangles. This work involves the use of bulldozers. Mr. Taylor at present has at his disposal only a handful of men and they are engaged on maintenance work, site clearing, and what Mr. Taylor describes as " Odds and Ends."

There is, however, one chance that some of the work can be begun in 1946. The main building of the College is scheduled as a national monument, and it is hoped that an application for a permit on these grounds will be successful.

UCL's Problem

This picture of the ruined Dome symbolises the extensive damage which is curtailing College activities.

Professor Richardson's plans for the rebuilding of the College are extensive. It is proposed to erect entirely new buildings along Gordon Street to replace the row of blitzed houses backing upon the College. Together with the existing main building and Dome, these buildings will bound two quadrangles. Within the last two years the College has purchased from the Duke of Bedford's Estate the whole site running from the Ramsay Memorial Laboratory to the corner of Gordon Square.

PHOTOELASTICITY : NEW SLANT ON CAMERA TECHNIQUE

Mr. Costa Mylonas, a post-graduate engineering student, is interested in the formation of a Photography Club. A native of Greece, Mr. Mylonas left Athens a few months ago to come to University College, where he is investigating Photoelasticity. Photo-elasticity is the study of the distribution of stresses in a structure by photographing transparent models in polarised light.

This research illustrates one of Mr. Mylonas' beliefs : that the art of photography can be combined with the science of Engineering to provide an invaluable research tool. In a recent statement, Mr. Mylonas said, " Now that peacetime conditions are gradually returning, there may be subjects you wish to photograph—an interestingly constructed bridge, a sunset, or even pages of a valuable manuscript you may wish to preserve photographically." Under present conditions of shortages, Mr. Mylonas feels, group work would be beneficial to all members of the group.

Any students who are interested in Mr. Mylonas' suggestion to start a Photography Club in University College, can contact him through the Engineering Beadle.

SIX UCL STUDENTS OFF TO SWITZERLAND

HALF-A-DOZEN students from University College are soon to set off for Switzerland under an exchange scheme with Swiss Universities. They are part of a contingent of about forty students of German from colleges all over the country. They are to go this April, and remain abroad six months. In their place, Swiss students are coming here to study English.

The first step in providing accommodation for the College after the return to its ruined buildings in 1945 was the construction of concrete huts in every available gap. Four were built in the Front Quad. Two were for the Union, which proposed naming them 'Cripps Cottage' and Bentham Bungalow': they were used for debates, chamber music concerts and a full range of revived student activities. Other huts in Foster Court and on the bomb-sites to the rear of the College, housed the Refectory, the Library and several academic departments. Once economic conditions permitted, the main building was finely restored and improved by Sir Albert Richardson, though it was not until 1951 that the General Library was re-opened and the building as a whole was only fully re-occupied in 1954.

355.

355. The main building in 1954 after its post-war restoration by Richardson, seen across the huts at the rear.

356. The architect who was responsible for most additions to the College buildings between the 1920s and the post-war reconstruction: Sir Albert Richardson, Professor of Architecture, 1919-46, photographed soon after his appointment.

357. H. O. Corfiato, Professor of Architectural Design, 1937-46, and of Architecture, 1946-60, photographed in the Common Room after the war.

356.

357.

358.

358. Richardson's design for a proposed new Gower Street entrance gate, part of the completely unrealised 1943 reconstruction plans.

359. The old Seamen's Hospital in Gordon Street, converted for the Union and the Department of Mathematics in 1959.

360. The houses on the west side of Gordon Square, the early Victorian culmination of Georgian Bloomsbury, all of which were gradually acquired by the College.

359.

360.

361. The last committee of the Women's Union Society prior to its amalgamation with the all-male Union Society to form 'the Union' in 1946; the members include Hannah Steinberg, who became Professor of Psychopharmacology in 1970.

361.

Despite all the material difficulties, the academic work of the College was rapidly resumed after the war. The great Tudor historian, Sir John Neale, Pollard's effective successor since 1927, powerfully continued to dominate the Department of History. His *Queen Elizabeth* (1934) remained one of the greatest and most popular of all historical biographies, painstakingly researched yet fresh. Neale was also a popular College figure – the first edition of the *UCL Student's Song Book* (1926) was dedicated to him. In other departments, new heads were appointed to build up their subjects: the philosopher A. J. Ayer, for example, and H. C. Darby, whose great work was the reconstruction of the geography of eleventh-century England from Domesday Book. A new Chair of Anthropology was established for Daryll Forde (see p. 203), but the Elliot Smith tradition of research was continued by N. A. Barnicot, who later became the country's first Professor of Physical Anthropology. In Town Planning, Lord Holford (as he was to become) succeeded Sir Patrick Abercrombie who had produced notable reports on the planning of Greater London; Holford himself was the planning consultant for the City of London's post-war rebuilding.

362.

362. Sir John Neale, FBA, Astor Professor of English History, 1927-56, photographed in the Senior Common Room in the late 1940s.

363. A. J. (later Sir Alfred) Ayer, FBA, Grote Professor of the Philosophy of Mind and Logic, 1946-59.

364. H. C. (later Sir Clifford) Darby, FBA, Professor of Geography, 1949-66.

365. N. A. Barnicot, Professor of Physical Anthropology, 1960-75, conducting his research.

363.

364.

365.

366.

366. Lord Holford, Professor of Town Planning, 1948-70, examining a model of St Paul's in connection with his scheme for rebuilding the war-damaged precincts.

367. The facsimile of an Elizabethan printing press originally built in the Department of English in 1932 by A. H. Smith and reconstructed after its war-time destruction, here being operated by Arthur Brown, Professor of English, 1962-69, and of Library Studies, 1969-73.

368. A colophon from the printing press in the Department of English.

367.

369.

368.

369. L. A. Willoughby (second from left), Priebsch's successor in the Chair of German in 1931, at a party marking his retirement in 1950, with Elizabeth M. Wilkinson, FBA (left), herself Professor of German, 1960-76, and W. Schwarz (second from right), later also Professor of German, 1964-72. A student at the College first in 1902, Willoughby was elected a Fellow of the College in 1910, and was the Senior Fellow at the time of his death aged 92 in 1977.

In 1951, Pye, ill, retired as Provost. He was succeeded by Sir Ifor Evans, who was destined to preside over the College in a period which saw rapid growth and change on an even greater scale than that witnessed in the Gregory Foster era. Sir Ifor Evans had himself first been a student of English at the College in 1917, and he had led an active subsequent career as Professor of English at Southampton and Sheffield, as Education Director of the British Council during the war, as Principal of Queen Mary College after it. For fifteen years he was to devote himself to UCL and its many problems of overcrowding and rebuilding at a time when national policy was demanding still further expansion. He faced all the difficulties fairly and firmly, and with a patience, tact and charm that minimised the disappointments following difficult decisions. He did this while remaining a well-known literary critic, writer, broadcaster and also serving the Arts Council, the *Observer* and a good many other advisory bodies. Swift of dispatch and easy of access, he was not only much admired in the College, but also much loved.

370. Sir Ifor Evans, later Lord Evans of Hungershall, the fourth Provost, 1951-66, as painted by Sir William Coldstream. The portrait took seventy-three meticulous sittings spread over two years, and Evans later confessed that he had wondered if he would live to see it completed. At the presentation following the eventual completion in 1960, Evans reminisced about meeting his wife at the College over forty years previously 'when I looked a little younger, and if I may venture to say so, a little more cheerful than when Professor Coldstream got to work on me'.

371. A characteristic view of the College buildings during the Evans era – the Physics Building (opened in 1953, and completed in 1959) and the New Refectory (opened in 1961), seen across some of the ever-present huts, some of which were later demolished to make way for the Central Collegiate Building, and the rest of which are being demolished in 1990.

371.

372.

372. Building underway to create the New Refectory, fashioned by Richardson out of what had originally been called the Brundrett Wing when built by Donaldson in 1849 (see 91.), seen beyond the back of the old Birkbeck Laboratory (see 87.)

373. The interior of the New Refectory under construction.

373.

In the fine 'testimonial' presented to Sir Ifor Evans on his retirement in 1966, signed by nearly a thousand of his colleagues, he was addressed as 'an outstanding benefactor to the College, not only by your power to shape and order its affairs, but, to a singular degree, by being the cause of benefactions in others'. The government, through the war damage compensation and through the University Grants Committee, provided substantial sums for the acquisition of property and for new buildings. But a good deal of the money for the expansion of the 1950s and 1960s had to come in the traditional way through appeals and gifts. In Evans's day this flow was faster than ever. The first appeal, coinciding with the centenary of Sir William Ramsay's birth, provided for a new storey on the Chemistry building. The second brought in £400,000 from industry for the Engineering Building on Torrington Place. Lord Marks gave £160,000 towards a new refectory and the start of the Central Collegiate Building; Lord Samuel gave another £100,000; the Wolfson Foundation gave generously too, and through these and other benefactions the College's facilities and its accommodation for students began to be revolutionised.

374.

374. The New Refectory in use soon after its opening in 1961.

375. The Lower Refectory extended later in the brutal concrete of the post-Richardson phase of the College's rebuilding.

375.

376. The Biological Sciences Building under construction in 1959. It was opened in 1964, and involved the demolition of a number of a number of Gower Street houses. One had belonged to Lady Diana Cooper; the murals by Rex Whistler (a Slade student in the 1920s) portraying the goddess Diana were moved from the house to the College in 1960, and have since graced the Refectory's Whistler Room.

376.

377.

377. Another of the demolished houses in Gower Street had been occupied by Darwin, as the blue plaque continues to testify on the Darwin Building, as the building was re-named in 1982 on the occasion of the centenary of Darwin's death.

378.

379.

378. The steel framework under construction for the large new Engineering Building designed by Corfiato.

379. The Engineering Building soon after its opening in 1961.

381.

382.

383.

380. The Department of Mathematics in 1949, when Massey was still its head; the photograph includes, among many who were to achieve considerable scientific distinction, eight who were to become professors of UCL: M. J. Seaton, FRS (extreme right of front row), T. Estermann (third from left, second row), L. Castillejo (first from left, third row), E. H. S. Burhop, FRS (fourth from left, second row), C. A. Rogers, FRS (third from right, second row), Sir Robert Boyd, FRS (third from left, top row), K. Roth, FRS (sixth from left, top row) and E. A. Power (seventh from left, top row).

381. Sir Harrie Massey, FRS, was one of the most outstanding of many scientists at UCL who during the post-war years achieved fame not only through research but through shaping leading departments in their fields. He came to UCL as Goldsmid Professor of Mathematics, 1938-1950, and was then translated to the Department of Physics as Quain Professor, 1950-1975, serving also as Vice-Provost, 1969-1973.

382. Dame Kathleen Lonsdale, FRS, the crystallographer, Professor of Chemistry, 1949-68 – one of the first two women to be elected to the Fellowship of the Royal Society (in 1945), and the first woman to become a professor at UCL.

383. E. S. Pearson, FRS, Professor of Statistics, 1935-60, the son of Karl Pearson and one of the three men it took to succeed 'K. P.' in his various fields.

384. J. Z. Young, FRS, Professor of Anatomy, 1945-74, photographed receiving a stuffed octopus presented by students on his retirement; his remarkably productive work on the mechanisms of memory using the creatures continued long after his retirement.

384.

385.

386.

387.

388.

389.

385. The first of four more leading scientists who headed distinguished departments: Sir Christopher Ingold, FRS, Professor of Chemistry, 1930-61.

386. D. Hughes, FRS, Professor of Chemistry, 1948-63.

387. E. N. da C. Andrade, FRS, Quain Professor of Physics, 1928-50.

388. Sir Peter Medawar, CH, FRS, Jodrell Professor of Zoology and Comparative Anatomy, 1951-62, who was awarded the Nobel Prize for Physiology or Medicine in 1960.

389. The gathering of distinguished physiologists outside the Department of Physiology on the occasion of the retirement of Sir Charles Lovatt Evans, FRS, in 1949.

The Faculty of Arts has followed a rather different course from Science in the last generation. Its present total of twenty-one Departments vary considerably in size, and it has achieved far less coherence: most of the Departments have gone over to the course-unit system or at least College-based degrees, while others have retained the traditional University-based final examination, together with intercollegiate teaching. Above all, it has to a great extent retained the tradition of individual rather than group research projects. Something of its story can be indicated through some of its more prominent members.

T. B. L. Webster, a brilliant and prolific writer on the relations of art and literature in ancient Greece, was the founder of the University's Institute of Classical Studies; he takes credit also for offering Michael Ventris his only academic post as Honorary Research Associate in Greek after his revolutionary discovery that Linear B tablets were written in an early form of Greek.

390.

Pylos 1952 No 641

ti-ri-po-de ai-ke-u ke-re-si-jo we-ke
τρίποδε

ti-ri-po e-me po-de o-wo-we
τρίπος

ti-ri-po ke-re-si-jo we-ke a-pu ke-ka-u-me-no ke-re-a₂
τρίπος   ἀπυκεκαυμένος σκέλεα ·

qe-to

di-pa me-zo-e! qe-to-ro-we   4 !
δίπας μέζον κʷετρ-ῶϝες ·

di-pa-E me-zo-e ti-ri-o-we-e   3 !
δίπα'ε μέζο'ε τρι-ώϝε'ε

di-pa me-wi-jo qe-to-ro-we   4 !
δίπας μέϝιον κʷετρ-ῶϝες ·

di-pa me-wi-jo ti-ri-jo-we   3 !
δίπας μέϝιον τρι-ῶϝες ·

di-pa me-wi-jo a-no-we   0 !
δίπας μέϝιον ἀν-ῶϝες

390. One of Michael Ventris's work-charts in his own hand, used in his pioneering study of Linear B texts, now preserved in the Institute of Classical Studies.

391. T. B. L. Webster, FBA, Professor of Greek, 1948-67.

391.

392. C. Daryll Forde, FBA, Professor of Anthropology, 1945-69.

393. A. D. Momigliano, KBE, FBA, Professor of Ancient History, 1951-75.

394. A. B. C. Cobban, Professor of French History, 1953-68.

395. A cartoon of Brian Woledge, Fielden Professor of French Language and Literature, 1939-71, the first Englishman to hold a chair of French in London.

394.

395.

Daryll Forde, originally a geographer who migrated to prehistoric archaeology and thence to social anthropology, created a Department of Anthropology which reflects in its structure his own range of interests; it is unique in offering to undergraduates courses in material culture as well as both physical and social anthropology. In French, Brian Woledge was the man responsible for widening the Department's range to include Renaissance and twentieth-century studies; his own work on early medieval literature was a pioneering application of computer analysis to the study of medieval texts. The Department of History developed an impressive range of interests. Following Pollard's footsteps, two more specialised Institutes were generated in the 1960s – for Latin American Studies, inspired by R. A. Humphreys, the first Professor of Latin American History, and for United States Studies, under H. C. Allen, Hale Bellot's successor as Commonwealth Fund Professor of American History. Alfred Cobban, a member of the Department from 1937 until his death in 1968 dealt lucidly and memorably with modern French history and political ideas. The widest interests of all were those of A. D. Momigliamo, whose prodigious writings weave a powerful counterpoint between the ancient world and the modern, between ideas and social reality, between historical problems and their historiography.

396. Reg Butler teaching sculpture in the Slade.

397. Sir William Coldstream, Slade Professor of Fine Art, 1949-75.

398. The Slade Antique Room, which was abolished in the 1960s.

396.

397.

398.

Sir William Coldstream, Slade Professor from 1949 to 1975, had been a Slade student himself in the late twenties and then, after a period in film production, joined with Claude Rogers and Victor Pasmore to found the influential Euston Road School in 1937. As a painter, he is best known for portraits showing that scrupulous concern for empirical observation which is the hall-mark of the Slade tradition. As Professor, however, tolerance and open-mindedness were the key words and the School's work broadened to include new studies and a wider range of styles and experiments. Sculpture already had an established tradition, to which Reg Butler as Director of Studies between 1966 and 1981 added: but amongst the developments in Coldstream's time were postgraduate work in many areas, film studies, and the facilities for wood, metal, and photographic work and the extension of a full range of print-making facilities. Meanwhile, as a committee man of wholly individual and quite devastating style, he became widely known and loved inside the College, and extremely influential in art education outside it. It was in fact the Coldstream Report on art education which led inside College as elsewhere to the expansion of art history teaching in the 1960s. The first Professor of the History of Art to become full-time – his part-time predecessors included Sir Ernst Gombrich – was L. D. Ettlinger in 1964: he it was who created six joint-degrees with Art History and set up

399.

400.

the independent Department which expanded dramatically under Professor John White between 1971 and 1990.

In 1965 the College, with help from the Max Rayne Foundation, acquired the old offices in Endsleigh Gardens of the National Union of General and Municipal Workers. The building was given to the Faculty of Laws, which had been expanding rapidly and was previously inadequately housed in the Torrington Place building. Today, it is one of the strongest areas of College in terms of student demand for places. It maintains traditional interests in jurisprudence and Roman Law, but has also been in the forefront of new developments in the undergraduate teaching of law: between 1967 and 1986 it posessed the only Professor of Air and Space Law; it was the first in the country to develop courses for undergraduates on International Air Law and Economic Law and the first to offer options in Russian and Soviet Law, using these as a vehicle for the comparative study of law, and new Chairs in Japanese Law and in the Law of Media of Communications and Expression (the Goodman Chair) have recently been established. The Faculty also cooperates in the large interogative Master's programme, particularly in the field of European Community law studies.

399. The present Laws building in Endsleigh Gardens, purchased in 1965 and previously the offices of the General and Municipal Workers, now re-named Bentham House.

400. The moot room of the Faculty of Laws, which contributes an important element to the experience of undergraduate lawyers, seen with Professor Jeffrey L. Jowell, Professor of Public Law since 1975, in the judicial seat.

401.

401. Bentham Hall, converted out of houses in Cartwright Gardens, provided a hall of residence for men students between 1952 and 1973.

402. Ifor Evans – Lord Evans of Hungershall – photographed outside Ifor Evans Hall on the occasion of its opening in 1968. It now provides accommodation for over 320 students, while Max Rayne House, on the same site in Camden Town, provides for a further 295.

402.

The growth of student accommodation at UCL is one of its greatest successes since the war. In 1947 there were 47 student places available; by 1961 there were 350, and 1,500 by 1978. Today the College provides over 2,000 places in halls of residence or student houses, with 150 further places under construction, apart from nearly 500 students living in the 'intercollegiate' halls of the University.

From 1952, Bentham Hall for men and from 1954 Campbell Hall for women, provided 250 places between them through the conversion of existing properties not far from the College site. A breakthrough came in 1961, when the College became the first university institution to attempt the provision of self-catering houses for students, first in Gordon Street and later in Bedford Way. But the long-term solution was to be found in purpose-built halls and a series of extraordinary benefactions made the programme possible. The 'Anonymous Donor' provided for Ramsay Hall, the first phase of which was opened in 1964, and for Ifor Evans Hall, opened in 1968. Lord Samuel gave the air-space above a block of shops in Oxford Street for the building of Goldsmid House, also opened in 1968. Meanwhile, the Max Rayne Foundation gave £50,000 a year for ten years to support the building programme and in particular the building of Max Rayne House, opened in 1970.

404.

405.

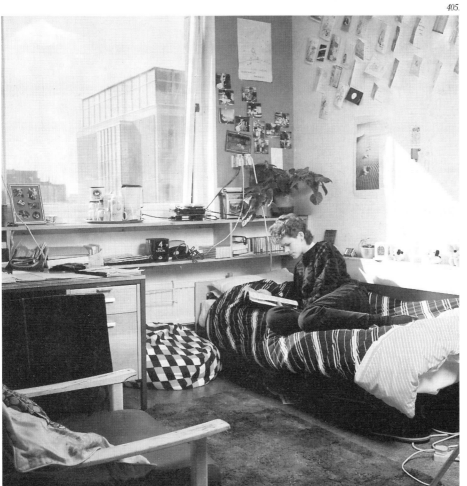

403. *Ramsay Hall photographed in 1987 just before the opening of the third phase of its building, showing the second phase (right) opened in 1971 and the original building (left) opened in 1964. It now provides accommodation for nearly 400 students, a few minutes walk from the College rectangle.*

404. *Goldsmid House in Oxford Street, opened in 1968 as UCL's first purpose-built self-catering 'student house' (as distinct from a hall of residence, which provides communal meals). There are 134 single study bedrooms and 12 kitchens, as well as lounges, computer terminals, a music room and a launderette.*

405. *A student in her room in Astor College, opened in 1967 as the Middlesex Hospital Medical School residence, which since the amalgamation to create the University College and Middlesex School of Medicine in 1987, has formed part of the College's extensive stock of student accommodation.*

406. Lord Annan, the fifth Provost, 1966-78, photographed at his desk.

407. The New Chemistry Building under construction in Gordon Street shortly before its completion in 1969, with (left) the Endsleigh Hotel, later demolished to make way for Wates House.

408. The Chemistry Building houses the Christopher Ingold Laboratories and the commemorative plaque recording that they were opened by Sir Christopher Ingold in 1970 was in fact unveiled by Lady Ingold, owing to his indisposition. She is accompanied by the then Head of Department, Sir Ronald Nyholm, FRS, later tragically killed in a car accident in 1971, at the height of a career of most productive research and outstanding administration.

Noël Annan came to UCL in 1966 from Cambridge where he had been a lecturer in politics since 1948 and Provost of King's College since 1956. He became a Life Peer in 1965. A formidable reputation as scholar, administrator and orator preceded him, though it took the College time to adjust to a profound change of style from that of his predecessor. Events were to sharpen the contrast between the two periods, as the years of the expansion gave way to economies, frozen posts and competition for diminishing funds. The years which followed required above all skilled diplomacy, not only to deal with severe cuts in establishment, but with the threat of student unrest and with far-reaching changes in the organisation and role of the College's non-academic staff. In 1966, as in 1951, the College was fortunate in finding the right man to deal with the problems of the time.

The momentum of expansion continued for a while: the Central Collegiate Building and its Theatre were opened in 1968; the first stage of the new Chemistry Building was completed in 1969 and formally opened as the Christopher Ingold Laboratories in 1970 for teaching purposes, though the old Chemistry Laboratories of 1915 continued to be used for research until the top floor was added to the new building in 1984. The Student Health Service, founded in 1945 and inadequately housed in Gower Street until 1973, received a new building thanks to a benefaction from the Wolfson Trust. The last major building of the Annan years was Wates House, built through a substantial donation from the Wates Foundation and opened in 1975 as a new home for the Bartlett School of Architecture and Planning.

406.

407.

408.

409.

410.

411.

409. The Health Centre, opened in 1973.

410. Wates House, opened in 1975 by Sir Ronald Wates, to house the Bartlett School of Architecture and Planning, later the Bartlett School of Architecture, Building, Environmental Design and Planning, which since 1969 has also been the Faculty of Environmental Studies.

411. The pavilion of the Union's sports-ground at Shenley.

UCL continued to be the home for many distinguished scientists and engineers. For a long time, the College had the unusual distinction of having two Nobel prize-winners in Physiology or Medicine on the academic staff. In Engineering, the chair of Photogrammetry and Surveying established in 1946 was the only one of its kind in the country; the separate department was created in 1961 under E. H. Thompson, who held the chair from 1951 until his death in 1976. Mechanical Engineering had been a separate department since the restructuring of the Faculty after the war; with Professor R. E. D. Bishop at the helm from 1957 to 1981, it developed particular interests concerned with the sea and the Navy, as the pre-war emphasis on photo-elasticity and the study of bodies at rest swung towards dynamics and the management of vibration. In 1967 the Department took over from the Royal Naval College at Greenwich the teaching for the Royal Corps of Naval Constructors, resulting in the creation of a very successful postgraduate course, based on a radical reappraisal of naval architecture. The first British postgraduate course in Ocean Engineering followed in 1972, established with an eye to the need for specialist engineers caused by the exploitation of the North Sea for gas and oil.

The Department of Physics and Astronomy was formed by amalgamation in 1972, establishing the largest and most far-flung of all College departments. The Observa-

412. The Observatory at Mill Hill, taken over by UCL when the Department of Astronomy was set up in 1951, having been originally built to house a 24-inch reflector presented to the University in 1928, with a second dome added in 1938. The modern successors of these are still in use for both research and undergraduate teaching.

413. Holmbury St Mary, near Dorking, where the Mullard Space Science Laboratory has been housed since 1966, when a donation from Mullard Ltd made possible the adaptation of a country mansion, Holmbury House.

414. The 'back-up' version of Ariel 1, the satellite launched in 1962 as a result of Anglo-American co-operation. It is now on display at Holmbury St. Mary.

412.

413.

414.

415.

p.e.c. fermenter

416.

417.

tory at Mill Hill had been part of the College since 1951; space research had begun in the Department of Physics in 1956 when a group led by R. L. F. (later Sir Robert) Boyd was set up. As a result of the successful launch of the Ariel 1 satellite in 1962, it became one of the most powerful research groups in Britain, taking full advantage of the American space research programme.

Sir Harrie Massey (see *381.*) was the instigator of this, as well as of other research groups including a particularly fertile one concerned with particle physics. Later, working as part of the European Organisation for Nuclear Research (CERN) at Geneva, fundamental discoveries were made about a range of elementary particles and the 'weak neutral current force'.

419.

418.

418. Sir Eric Turner, FBA, Professor of Papyrology, 1950-78, the only professor of the subject in the country at the time; it was he who inspired and organized the methodical publication of the papyri from Oxyrrhynchus in Egypt and so transformed our knowledge, for example, of the comic playwright Menander of Athens, whose works had been lost since antiquity.

419. A fragment from Menander's play, the Samia.

420. A speech therapist and a child using speech pattern displays developed in the Department of Phonetics and Linguistics for training in voice production and control. Much progress was made from the 1970s towards the transmission of voice information to totally deaf patients.

420.

421.

421. The Survey of Spoken English (now re-named the Survey of English Usage), one of the College's major research projects, arrived together with its originator Professor (later Sir) Randolph Quirk, FBA, from Durham in 1960. Its purpose is to provide a corpus of 'the grammatical repertoire of adult educated speakers of British English', using the evidence both of written and spoken language. The project continues today, having survived the departure of its first Director to be Vice-Chancellor of the University; its second Director is Professor Sidney Greenbaum, Quain Professor of English Language and Literature, 1983-91.

422.

423.

422. Mary Douglas, Professor of Social Anthropology, 1970-78, seen in the setting of some of the symbols of ambivalence through which she explored the significance of classificatory systems, ancient and modern, thus challenging orthodoxies in many fields of learning.

423. The Flaxman casts (see p.69) in use for the teaching of Art History; the Department expanded rapidly in the course of the 1960s and 1970s, making the most of the many opportunities London offers for bringing classes face to face with the art of all periods.

424.

424. The administrative and library staff of the College assembled in 1955; the photograph includes 136 of the then total of about 200. The corresponding figure today would be about four times as great. Sir Ifor Evans as Provost sits in the centre; on his right is the Secretary of the College, 1947-64, E. A. L. Gueterbock, next to whom is the Assistant Secretary, 1948-68, Winifred Radley. Five places further along is L. J. Gue, at this time Publications Officer, who had already worked in the College for twenty-seven years; twenty-two years later, he retired as Deputy Secretary, having an unrivalled knowledge of the College's inner history in his time. On the Provost's left is J. W. Scott, who had been Librarian since 1954 and was to remain an unmistakeable figure in the College's life until his retirement in 1982; a fierce defender of the importance of scholarship and scholarly standards in the work of the Librarian, he is as well remembered for his skill in fighting his corner in the New Inn as in the Librarian's office.

Panora Ltd
Phone — CHANCERY 7779
56 Eagle Street,
London, W.C 1.

425. The 1977 photograph of the vigorous Department of Geography. Student life in UCL was and is based on the strong institution of the Department. The photograph illustrates how far dress and life-style had changed by the late 1970s compared to the immediate post-war years; those in ties can be assumed to be members of staff; those not in ties cannot necessarily be assumed to be students. Students of today may, however, find the modish flared trousers little less archaic than the frocks of 1955.

425.

426. The College Committee in session in July 1977. Under the terms of the new Charter later that year, it was to resume its nineteenth-century name of the College Council as well as its formal responsibility as the College's governing body. In the Chair is Sir Bernard Waley-Cohen, who had served as the Committee's Chairman since 1971 and before that as Treasurer, 1962-70, following a family tradition of service to UCL that had begun in the College's earliest days and continues today. On Sir Bernard's left is Arthur Tattersall, the Secretary of the College, 1964-78, a firm but humane administrator, strikingly successful in maintaining close relations between the administration and the College community; extreme right is the man who succeeded him in 1978, J. R. Tovell, who had been Finance Secretary since 1965.

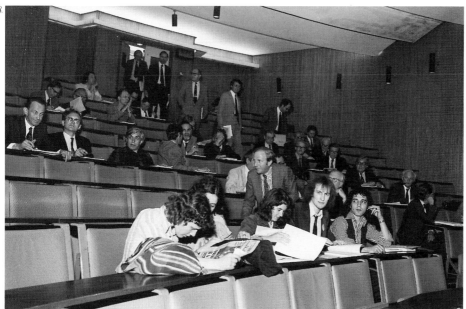

427. The strawberry tea in the Front Quad on the occasion of the Assembly of Faculties in 1962; this annual gathering occurred every year – apart from those of the second world war – between 1908 and 1966, when it was merged with the Union's Foundation week. It was revived between 1982 and 1988.

428. The Professorial Board assembling in June 1977. It too was re-named under the new Charter, becoming the Academic Board, but remained the controlling body on academic matters. All professors, a group of elected non-professors, and representatives of the student body comprised its membership. The students are here seen prominently in the foreground.

429.

430.

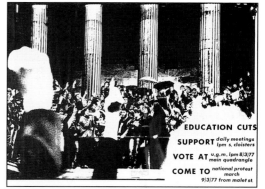

429. Allan Maccoll, Professor of Chemistry, 1963-81, and long-term supporter of the AUT, campaigning to 'rectify the anomaly' in a protest about the inadequacy of university teachers salaries in November 1977.

430. A poster protesting at cuts in government spending on education in March 1977; it shows the meeting in progress that resulted in a short sharp confrontation, in which the students occupied some administrative rooms for two days and the Slade School for rather longer. Such incidents have been very rare and peacefully resolved; the campaign against cuts by successive governments has continued intermittently ever since, but with little or no success.

The College received a new Royal Charter in November 1977, in succession to the Deed of Settlement of 1826, the first Charter of 1836, the Acts of Parliament of 1869 and 1905, and the University of London's Act of 1926, which had previously governed the College. The changes introduced by the 1977 Charter were largely formal and titular, but they restored the College's status as an independent corporation. The new Charter was twelve years in the making; if the old constitutional machinery had been put to any serious test during this time, 'the creaking would have been heard from here to Timbuctoo', said Arthur Tattersall, the Secretary of the College. As soon as it was granted, the 1977 Charter began to be revised to provide for the re-amalgamation with the Medical School.

The Queen Mother's visit in November 1977 marked the start of a series of celebrations for the sesquicentenary of the College, leading up to a great exhibition on 'UCL Past and Present' in May 1978, opened by Mrs Shirley Williams as Secretary of State for Education. The sesquicentenary was celebrated confidently, but it was a time of increasing financial uncertainty for universities in general and for London colleges in particular.

431. The Queen Mother, as Chancellor of the University, receiving one of the early prints of the College from Sir Bernard Waley-Cohen and Lord Annan during her visit in November 1977 to accept an Honorary Fellowship of the College.

432. The Royal Charter issued to the College in November 1977.

431.

ELIZABETH THE SECOND

by the Grace of God of the United Kingdom of Great Britain and Northern Ireland and of Our other Realms and Territories Queen, Head of the Commonwealth, Defender of the Faith:

TO ALL TO WHOM THESE PRESENTS SHALL COME, GREETING!

WHEREAS an humble Petition has been presented unto Us by Our most dearly beloved Mother Queen Elizabeth The Queen Mother, Chancellor of Our University of London, Sir Cyril Philips, then Vice-Chancellor of Our University of London and by the College Committee of University of London, University College: praying that We should grant a Charter of Incorporation for the purpose of re-constituting University of London, University College as a College of the University of London:

AND WHEREAS We have taken the said Petition into Our Royal Consideration and are minded to accede thereto:

NOW THEREFORE KNOW Ye that We by virtue of Our Prerogative Royal and of Our especial grace, certain knowledge and mere motion have willed and ordained and by these Presents do for Us, Our Heirs and Successors will and ordain as follows:—

1. University of London, University College is hereby re-constituted as a college of the University of London by the name and style of "University College London", hereinafter referred to as "the College".

2. The Council, the Academic Board, the Fellows and Honorary Fellows, the Academic Staff and Students of the College and all such other persons as may pursuant to this Our Charter and the Statutes and Regulations of the College become Members of the Body Corporate are hereby constituted and shall for ever hereafter be one Body Corporate and Politic by the name of "University College London" with perpetual succession and a Common Seal.

3. The objects of the College shall be to provide education and courses of study in the fields of Arts, Laws, Pure Sciences, Medicine and Medical Sciences, Social Sciences and Applied Sciences and in such other fields of learning as may from time to time be decided upon by the College and to encourage research in the said branches of knowledge and learning and to organise, encourage and stimulate postgraduate study in such branches.

4. The College, subject to this Our Charter and to the Statutes and Regulations of Our University of London (hereinafter referred to as "the University") shall in furtherance of the foregoing objects but not otherwise have the following powers:—

(1) To take over from the University the properties and liabilities hitherto entrusted to vested in or incurred by the University on behalf of the College by virtue of its incorporation in the University.

(2) To provide courses of instruction and facilities for research in the branches of knowledge and learning mentioned in Article 3 of this Our Charter, and for postgraduate study in such branches.

(3) To provide, maintain, alter and improve for the use of the Students

In 1978 Lord Annan resigned as Provost in order to become the first full-time Vice-Chancellor of the University of London in preparation for the constitutional changes brought about the University's new 1978 Act of Parliament. For the following academic year, 1978-79, Professor Harold Billett was Acting Provost. He had been a member of the staff since 1946, Professor of Mechanical Engineering from 1965, and a Vice-Provost since 1973. Professor Billett presided calmly and wisely over the College in an inter-regnum between two contrasting commanding Provosts.

Sir James Lighthill was chosen as Provost in 1979. Like Lord Annan, he came to UCL from Cambridge with a formidable, but utterly different, reputation. He was a brilliant mathematician, Lucasian Professor of Applied Mathematics at Cambridge at the time of his appointment, a product of Winchester and Trinity College, Cambridge, who had been a professor at Manchester at 26, an FRS at 29, and Director of the Royal Aircraft Establishment at Farnborough from 1959 to 1964. As Provost, he found, as he put it, 'something of an advantage' in being an applied mathematician who worked for many years on various applications of mathematics in the sciences, in engineering, and in medicine. There were few academic subjects in which he did not have some expertise, and there were no areas of the College on which he did not have considerable impact in the nine years that he devoted to the College. In 1988, Sir James Lighthill expressed the hope that the history of the College in the 1980s would be judged by the quality of the professorial appointments made during his Provostship, over a hundred of them altogether. He put academic excellence first, but he had many other problems to deal with.

In 1979-80 there had to be a savings target of 3% of the recurrent grant from the UGC, and there were various problems arising from the UGC insistence on non-EEC students being charged fees on a new higher level. What the *Annual Report* called a 'traumatic sequence of body-blows' followed in 1980-81, especially following the government decision announced in the 1981 budget to cut substantially the resources provided for the university system as a whole. The College found its grant for 1981-82 revealed a shortfall of 15% in the amount needed to maintain the 1980-81 level of activity. Retrenchment was not easy, given that nearly 80% of College expenditure was on staff. Sir James Lighthill was obliged to introduce a 'seven-point plan' for economies, and to hammer out painful plans for coping with the cuts. A firm 'no redundancy' policy was adopted, but an extensive early retirement scheme was introduced, with a target of 160 members of the academic staff by 1984.

The target was achieved (though for many academics, it was a retirement only on paper) and substantial one-off as well as on-going economies were made in various different ways, while at the same time the College embarked on a vigorous drive to increase its income from non-governmental sources. Industry as well as the research councils and charitable foundations were

433.

H. A. Freeth '80

433. *Professor Harold Billett,
Acting Provost, 1978-79, in a
portrait by H. A. Freeth hanging in
the Housman Room.*

434. *Sir James Lighthill, FRS, the
sixth Provost of the College,
1979-89, photographed in his office
soon after taking up his
appointment, holding a copy of
one of his important contributions
to the field of fluid dynamics.*

increasingly turned to. In a period of
enormous financial difficulties, the College
was so successful in obtaining alternative
sources of funding that the number of staff
in academic departments actually in-creased from 1,976 in 1978-79 to 2,014 in
1982-83. Beginning with the 'massive cuts'
of the beginning of the decade, the 1980s
turned out to be a remarkable period of
expansion for the College.

Some of UCL's expansion derived from the intense period of 'restructuring' which the University of London embarked upon under the Vice-Chancellorships of Lord Annan, 1978-81, and his successor, Professor Sir Randolph Quirk, 1981-85. The report by Lord Flowers in 1980 on medical education in the University was followed by an investigation into the organisation of all other subjects conducted by Sir Peter Swinnerton-Dyer, later Chairman of the UGC. A period of anguish and mergers ensued, coinciding with the 'cuts'. For many parts of the University it was dismaying and hurtful, but UCL was on the whole a beneficiary.

In 1982-83, a number of geologists were translated from Queen Mary College to enhance the Department of Geology (from 1985 re-named Geological Sciences) under Professor Michael Audley-Charles; Bedford College's Department of Dutch moved to the College *en bloc*; the Department of Italian was strengthened by transfers from Bedford, as was the Department of Mathematics, which came to include Professor P. M. Cohn, FRS, as well as Dr Bill Stephenson.

Complex discussions with Westfield College did not lead to a merger, but in 1986 the Institute of Archaeology – a close neighbour, though an independent institute of the University – amalgamated with the College, retaining its separate identity within the Faculty of Arts.

The Bioengineering Centre in the Department of Mechanical Engineering was established in 1980, after the transfer from Roehampton of a DHSS group integrating engineering and medical research. The D. M. S. Watson Library, after 're-structuring' of University library provision, became the Bloomsbury Science Library in 1985. But the biggest changes of all were in medicine. In April 1980 the University College Hospital Medical School – a separate school of the University since 1907 (see p.136) – was re-united with the College, forming the Faculty of Clinical Sciences within a new UCL School of Medicine. Soon afterwards negotiations began towards a further amalgamation with the Middlesex Hospital School of Medicine, a development achieved by November 1987 when the 'University College and Middlesex School of

435.

Medicine' was inaugurated. It included three formerly separate institutes, the Institute of Urology, the Institute of Orthopaedics and the Institute of Laryngology and Otology. The enlarged UCL came to contain over 7,000 students.

During this period of expansion, the College acquired a new look. In 1979-80, the stone-cleaning of the Front Quad improved the outward appearance of the College dramatically, and in 1983-85 the Front Quad was closed to enable the building of a new main front entrance. The unsightly post-war huts were finally removed, and the College came to present a handsome front to the world. The Kathleen Lonsdale Building, containing the old chemistry laboratories, was elegantly reconstructed in 1985 to house the Sandoz Institute for Medical Research – a signal example of cooperation with a major pharmaceutical company – and all these changes combined with some modest gardening expenditure as part of a 'greening of UCL' programme to significantly improve the rectangle site, what Sir James Lighthill liked to call the 'half-kilometre square'.

435. The Sesquicentenary Appeal, delayed in the hope of better times to come, was finally launched in October 1981 in the presence of HRH Princess Anne on the day that she was installed as Chancellor of the University of London in succession to the Queen Mother. Here Sir James Lighthill as Provost presents Lord Goodman, a Fellow of the College since 1965, who acted as Chairman of the Appeal; to the left of Princess Anne can be seen Professor Derrick James, Professor of Anatomy, 1970-86, Vice-Provost, 1978-84, who became Director of the Appeal.

436. In December 1981, Sir James Lighthill, holding a copy of the agreement with the Sandoz Pharmaceutical Co. to establish the Sandoz Institute for Medical Research at the College, receives a cheque from the officials of the company, gleefully watched (right) by John Tovell, Finance Secretary and Accountant, 1965-78, and Secretary of the College, 1978-82.

437. The centrepiece of the Appeal
launched in 1981 was the long
proposed 'filling of the gap' to
complete the Gower Street
entrance to the Front Quad. Sir
Hugh Casson's own elegant sketch
of the handsome pavilions he
conceived on either side of the
lodges was hung in the Royal
Academy's summer exhibition in
1981.

438. The view from the Portico in
1985 after the construction of the
two pavilions which completed the
Front Quad, the Pearson Building
to the north and the Chadwick
Building to the south, on either side
of the reconstructed lodges, with
Waterhouse's University College
Hospital towering beyond.

439. HM The Queen arriving at the
College on 13th November 1985
and being introduced to Ian Baker,
the retired general – formerly
Assistant Chief of the General Staff
for Operational Requirements and
General Officer Commanding
North-East District – who became
Secretary of the College in 1982.
Behind the Queen stands Dr Mary
Fulbrook, Lecturer in German
History, the then Mayoress of
Camden. Behind Ian Baker stands
Lord Donaldson, Master of the
Rolls and the College's Visitor
under the 1977 Charter.

440. The Queen entering through
the Portico accompanied by Sir
James Lighthill as Provost and Sir
Peter Matthews, Chairman of the
College Council, 1980-89.

441. The inscription above the
entrance in the Portico, as unveiled
by the Queen, records that the
Quadrangle begun in 1827 was
deemed complete in 1985. In her
speech in the Donaldson Library
she said: 'I confess that, sometimes,
when I lay a foundation stone I am
prey to faint worries about when,
or even whether, the building will
be finished. I wonder if, on that
April afternoon in 1827 when he
laid the first stone here, the Duke of
Sussex had those same worries.
Even if he did, I doubt if he would
have guessed that it would be his
great-great-grand niece, 158 years
later, who would see the end of the
process he began.'

441.

442. The Middlesex Hospital, founded in 1745 and rebuilt in 1935, had had its own Medical School since 1835, when it was inaugurated – as was the Faculty of Medicine at UCL – by Sir Charles Bell (see p.33). It was agreed that the Middlesex Hospital Medical School should amalgamate with the UCL Faculty of Clinical Sciences (as the former University College Hospital Medical School had become in 1980 when it re-united with the College) to create a new 'University College and Middlesex School of Medicine' within UCL. The first students were admitted to the Joint School in 1983 before the completion of the complex period of planning for full integration; projected for August 1987, the necessary Act of Parliament to give effect to this was delayed owing to the General Election of that year.

443. The formal inauguration of the University College and Middlesex School of Medicine was marked by the visit of HRH The Princess Royal – as Princess Anne had become – in November 1987. She spoke in the Edward Lewis Theatre in the presence of Professor D. V. I. Fairweather, Vice-Provost (Medical) and Head of the School (right of front row), Sir William Slack, the former Dean of the Middlesex Hospital Medical School who became Dean of the enlarged Faculty of Clinical Sciences (second from left, back row), and Professor A. P. Mathias, Dean of the Faculty of Medical Sciences (third from left, back row).

444. The first Grand Colours Dinner after the creation of the University College and Middlesex School of Medicine had on its cover the coats of arms and the mottos of the former University College Hospital Medical School and of the former Middlesex Hospital Medical School.

446.

446. The Institute of Archaeology, which merged with UCL in August 1986, having been founded in 1937 as an institute of the University of London by Sir Mortimer Wheeler (for whom see 205.). The leading centre for archaeological research as well as undergraduate teaching in the field, it has been housed in this building in Gordon Square since 1958.

447.

U C M S M

445. Soon afterwards a new logo was created for UCMSM, combining features from both the previous coats of arms.

445.

447. St Peter's Hospital in Covent Garden, established in 1860 to specialise in urological diseases, spawned the Institute of Urology as a research centre which in 1951 became one of the constituent parts of the British Postgraduate Medical Federation, itself a federal school of the University of London. The Institute of Urology along with two sister institutes – the Institute of Orthopaedics and the Institute of Laryngology and Otology – also joined the new UCMSM in 1987 as part of the enlarged UCL, bringing close connections with the Royal National Orthopaedic Hospital at Stanmore and the Royal National Throat Nose and Ear Hospital in Gray's Inn Road.

448. A group of powerful men: the Deans of the seven Faculties of UCL photographed on the Portico steps in 1986, together with the Provost, two Vice-Provosts and the Secretary of the College. Clockwise from Sir James Lighthill they are: Professor I. A. Harley, Dean of the Faculty of Engineering, Professor J. L. Jowell, Dean of the Faculty of Law; Professor D. Bishop, Dean of the Faculty of Environmental Studies, Professor A. P. Mathias, Dean of the Faculty of Medical Sciences, Professor John White, Vice-Provost, Professor J. W. Mullin, Vice-Provost, Mr I. H. Baker, the Secretary, Dr P. J. Verrill, Dean of the Faculty of Clinical Sciences, Professor R. J. Audley, Dean of the Faculty of Science and Professor M. M. Willcock, Dean of the Faculty of Arts. The financial problems of the 1980s have led to a significant increase in the power of the deans.

449. The title of Fellow of the College has been bestowed since 1842 on former students achieving distinction in their careers, whether academic or non-academic. Those chosen in 1982, shown here, include Dame Margaret Booth, a High Court Judge (sitting left) and Professor Eugenie Henderson, Professor of Phonetics at SOAS (sitting right), and (standing, left to right) Dr H. B. Wright, former Medical Adviser to the Institute of Directors, Prof H. O. Schild, Professor of Pharmacology, 1961-73, Professor M. A. Screech, Fielden Professor of French, 1971-84, Professor David Lodge, the novelist and Professor of English at Birmingham, Professor P. K. Thomas, Professor of Neurology at the Royal Free, John Eastwick-Field, the architect, Professor A. A. Glynn, Director of the Central Public Health Laboratory.

449.

450. The College Council photographed in March 1986, a month after a grand dinner was held to celebrate the 160th anniversary of the foundation of the College and the 150th anniversary of the establishment of the University of London. In the centre sits Sir Peter Matthews as Chairman of the Council, with Sir James Lighthill as Provost on his right and Ian Baker as Secretary on his left. Besides members of the academic staff, the Council contains lay members and student representatives.

450.

451.

451. A group of women: a photograph of the Academic Women's Advancement Group (AWAG), which has met in the College regularly since 1979 and is probably the oldest established women's academic group in the country. The time since its foundation has seen a substantial increase in the number of women professors at UCL, from four in 1979 to double-figures today, when some 13% of all women professors in the country are at UCL. In this photograph, Professor Hannah Steinberg, the Convenor of the Group, sits in the middle in front of the bookcase; sitting on the left is Lady Lighthill, and next to her Professor Laura Lepschy, Professor of Italian, with Professor Annette Lavers, Professor of French, standing behind her. Second from the right is Jacqueline Dyson, Senior Lecturer in Laws, and from 1990 Dean of Students.

452.

452. For many years, the totally inadequate stage in the gymnasium originally built for the Boys' School in 1878 had to serve for the many student dramatic productions, including the annual opera, a major feature of UCL life since 1951. The Music Society's policy has been to produce little-known operas and it has a number of premières to its credit. Since 1968 the operas have been staged in the first-class facilities of the Bloomsbury Theatre, employing aspiring professional singers in the main solo parts. The gym itself is finally to be pulled down in 1990-91 to make way for new buildings for medical research.

A history of an institution, especially one concerned with the creation and dissemination of knowledge, can all too easily give a spurious impression of continuity and of progress. Fundamental changes and discontinuities, especially ones not easy to illustrate, can be glossed over. Certainly the major theme in the College's history is that of growth, however difficult this was to achieve in the early years. The graph of student numbers exposes the most obvious fundamental change during the College's life. Besides the dramatic war-time falls of 1914-18 and 1939-45, the figures reveal three significant periods of growth: first, a period of modest growth between the late 1860s and the mid-1880s, following the initial period of stagnation; secondly, a period of rapid growth, interrupted by the first world war, from about 1900 to 1920, a period in which the College increased three-fold; and

453. The College's splendid Bloomsbury Theatre was opened in 1968 as the Collegiate Theatre, and re-named in 1982. In 1988 it was given a face-lift, with graphics designed by the cartoonist Gerald Scarfe. It provides facilities for student activities and performances, as well as for visiting professional groups.

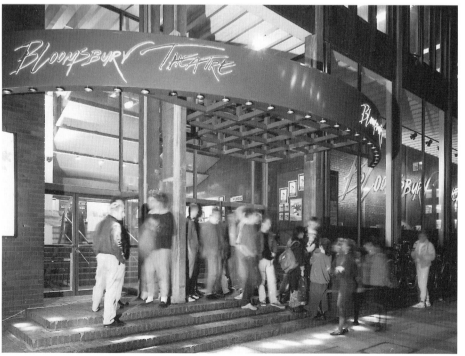

453.

thirdly, the last forty years, which have seen student numbers more than double.

Now there are over 9,000 students, about a third of them postgraduate or research students. There are over 1,700 members of the academic staff (nearly 800 of them UFC-funded, and the remainder grant and contract-funded), including no fewer than 191 professors. With administrative, secretarial, technical, library and support staff of all sorts, UCL now has a pay-roll of over 7,300. A College community totalling some 15,000 now use a complex of buildings on the original site and beyond. The annual expenditure is about £125 million. Much time has to be spent on managerial functions on a scale unknown in the nineteenth century. It is a far cry from the twenty-four professors of 1828, with

454.

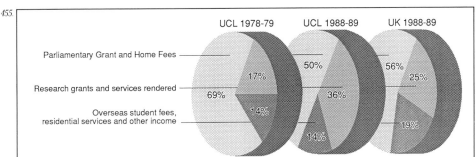

455.

their over-paid and underemployed Warden, one part-time Secretary and a single half-finished building.

There are major qualitative contrasts too. The College was the first to admit women to higher education on an equal basis with men, and this was in itself a revolutionary change. At the time of the foundation, the central purpose of the College was conceived as being teaching; the development of research as a parallel purpose – in some ways an over-riding purpose – has been one of the slow, silent revolutions. The founders, of course, sought men of originality and learning, who would add to the stock of knowledge, but what research they did was funded out of their own pockets. Only gradually did the College take responsibility for providing staff and facilities, and only gradually was a career structure built up for full-time academics. The nature of teaching itself has undergone transformation; 'while twenty years ago the bulk of the teaching work of the College

consisted of formal lectures', wrote Sir Gregory Foster in 1928, 'today, by a gradual process . . . the seminar, the discussion and tutorial class have been developed . . .' Teaching through discussion and individual laboratory work, the hall-marks of modern higher education, were not envisaged by the founders.

Public financing, sought by Ramsay in the 1880s and noted with concern by George V in 1927, grew after the first grant made in 1889, to become the predominant means of support in the age of mass higher education. The jolts of the last years of the UGC, and of the Universities Funding Council since 1989, have led to a reassessment of the system of financing. On many fronts, then, there have been deep changes, not least in the 1980s; but they are what Macaulay in 1826 called the 'details' which would vary with the necessities of every age (see pp.26-27); they do not weaken the continuing validity of the ideals of the founders, 'the spirit of its system'.

454. A graph showing the number of students registered at the College since the opening in 1828. Figures for women students are given separately from the first entry in 1878. Though there had been MA students from the 1840s, aggregate figures for postgraduates are available only from 1903, after which they too are given separately.

455. A diagram showing how substantial was the shift in the College's finances during the 1980s from dependence upon the UGC grant and home student fee income, together with the growth of income from industry and the research councils. In this period, the College's turnover increased from about £20 million per annum to over £100 million.

In two major national comparative investigations into research performance in British universities in the 1980s, UCL achieved remarkably high marks. In 1984-85 much energy was put into the task of depicting the research strengths of the College and defining research plans in response to a UGC 'research selectivity' investigation. Research profiles were drawn up for 24 subject areas, what the UGC called 'cost centres'. The research in 21 of them was judged 'better than average within the UK' by the UGC, and a total of 19 'stars' were awarded for outstanding performance, a result which placed UCL higher than any institution in the country other than Oxford or Cambridge.

A similar exercise was conducted by the UFC in 1989 and twenty departments were awarded the coveted top rating (a mark of 5), ratings awarded more sparingly than stars in 1986. All five departments in the Faculty of Engineering achieved the top rating, as did the Faculty of Laws, and the Departments of Physics and Astronomy, Computer Science, Anatomy, Physiology and Pharmacology in the Faculties of Science or Medical Science, and the Departments of History, Anthropology, 'Archaeology (including Egyptology)', Italian, Scandinavian Studies, Linguistics and the School of Library, Archive and Information Studies and the Slade School in the Faculty of Arts. Public recognition of the College's research achievements across many fields was thus unequivocally given, justifying Sir James Lighthill's vision of the College as a 'dynamic interacting cluster of centres of excellence'. This recognition bolstered the College as it continued to face increasingly stringent 'NEST' (New Earnings and Savings) targets in the late 1980s.

456. An artist's impression of the International Ultraviolet Explorer (IUE) Satellite, launched at Cape Canaveral in 1978, which for several years orbited the earth observing ultra violet radiation from astronomical objects of all kinds. The Department of Physics and Astronomy played a major role in its design.

457.

457. Professor Sir Robert Wilson, FRS, the current Head of the Department of Physics and Astronomy, with the prestigious award he received from President Ronald Reagan in 1988 for his leading contribution to the scientific programme of the International Ultraviolet Explorer Satellite.

458. A research student in the Department of Physics and Astronomy, Nick Wood, working on the forward detector of OPAL, the Omni Purpose Apparatus for the Large Electron-Positon Collider at CERN in Geneva in 1989, as the College's contribution to this research was about to produce remarkable results.

458.

459. Current research in high pressure fluidization in the Department of Chemical and Biochemical Engineering. The flow and stability of gas bubbles (shown in inset) are observed by X-rays in a unique facility, which is leading to important advances in knowledge which can be applied to the manufacture of gasoline, polymer intermediates and in pollution-free coal combustion units.

459.

460. Sir Lawrence Gowing, the Slade Professor of Fine Art, 1975-85, with one of his commanding canvasses.

461. Sir Randolph Quirk, FBA, Professor of English, 1960-81, and subsequently Vice-Chancellor of the University of London, photographed in his office in the College, watched over by a bust of his illustrious predecessor W. P. Ker (see p. 122).

462. Professor David Harris, Professor of Human Environment and Director of the Institute of Archaeology, photographed in the Institute's 'bone room', holding a skull of a dugong (sea cow) from the Torres Strait between Papua New Guinea and Australia.

463.

463. Professor R. E. D. Bishop FRS: Kennedy Professor of Mechanical Engineering, 1957-81, before becoming Vice-Chancellor of Brunel University.

464. Sir Eric Ash FRS: Pender Professor of Electrical Engineering, 1966-85, before becoming Rector of Imperial College.

465. Professor D. E. N. Davies FRS: Professor of Electrical Engineering, 1971-88, before becoming Vice-Chancellor of the Loughborough University of Technology.

464.

465.

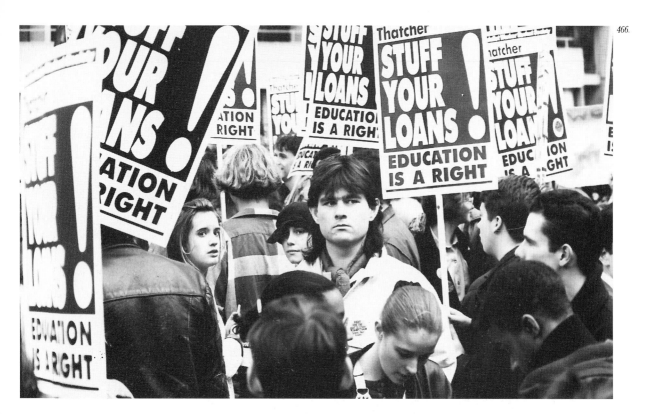

466.

466. *A photograph (by courtesy of Pi) that provides an image of the 1980s.*

467. *Another image (also by courtesy of Pi) that reveals the increasing complexity of the College in the 1980s, evidently as far as students are concerned.*

468. *The plan of the College as appended to the 'Institutional Plan' submitted to the UFC in 1990. The 'rectangle' includes the north-western corner site of Lewis's bookshop, recently acquired for the College, and shows the sites on and off the 'rectangle' currently identified for development. The present University College Hospital is marked as 'future library', highlighting the most significant of all possibilities for the future.*

467.

Proposed New Buildings

1. Centre for Biochemical Engineering
2. Proposed Eisai Institute
3. Teaching/Conference Centre
4. Molecular Cell Biology IRC
5. Conservation Centre for Archaeology
6. Academic Space

In April 1989 Dr Derek Roberts, FRS, was chosen to succeed Sir James Lighthill as Provost, an appointment that attracted much attention in the press, especially since the AUT was threatening a boycott of examination marking following the government's refusal to make an adequate salary settlement on top of its insistence upon abolition of 'tenure' by legislation. Dr Roberts had held several visiting professorships (including one in the College's Department of Electronic and Electrical Engineering), but he was not an academic. His life had been spent in industrial scientific research and at the time of his appointment as Provost he was Joint Deputy Managing Director and Technical Director of GEC. The appointment, welcomed throughout the College, was seen as a sign of the times.

The times were indeed changing. An exhaustive report in 1985 in connection with Sir Alex Jarratt's investigation of the efficiency of universities had pronounced 'the overall governance of UCL, in terms of its organisational structure and decision processes, is generally effective'. A new managerial and public relations style was becoming evident. David Bowles, the College's Finance Secretary and Accountant since 1978 became Director of Finance and Planning in 1989; an Alumnus Day was held on an entirely new basis; *UCL Universe* replaced the old *Annual Report*, and a glossy news-magazine, UCL NEWS, was launched. Some of these developments had been foreshadowed before 1989. Dr Stephen Montgomery had been appointed Director of External Relations in 1985, and in 1988 the former ASU (Academic Services Unit, established in 1978) had been re-launched as UCLi, UCL Initiatives, a concerted effort to link UCL expertise to industrial and commercial opportunities. UCLv, UCL Ventures, a company with access to venture capital, was to follow. By the end of 1990, major new buildings were underway. UCL chose not to sit on its laurels.

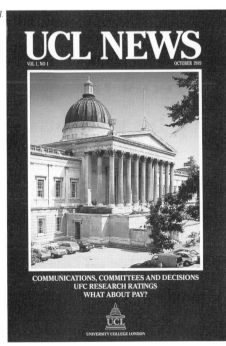

469. Dr Derek Roberts FRS, the seventh Provost from April 1989, seen here shaking hands with his predecessor, Sir James Lighthill, in front of a portrait of Jeremy Bentham.

470. The building-site at the back of the main building in December 1990, with the post-war huts finally removed, in preparation for the construction of the new Advanced Centre for Biochemical Engineering, adjoining the new Eisai Research Laboratory for Molecular Biology and the new IRC Cell Biology building.

471. The cover of the first issue of UCL NEWS in October 1989, one of the signs of the effort the College is making to polish up its self-image.

ACKNOWLEDGEMENTS

A work such as this is naturally one which has involved the co-operation of a good many colleagues, both past and present. It is a revised version of the first edition, produced at the time of the sesquicentenary of the College in 1978, expanded and brought up to date. In re-approaching our task, we are grateful for the enthusiasm of Professor John White, Pro-Provost, and Dr Stephen Montgomery, Director of External Affairs. To our gratitude for the original support given by Arthur Tattersall, the then Secretary of the College, who gave his immediate backing to the idea of such a history, and by Lord Annan, the then Provost, J. W. Scott, the then Librarian and J. R. Tovell, the then Finance Secretary, we add our gratitude to Sir James Lighthill and Dr Derek Roberts, successive Provosts, Ian Baker, the present Secretary, Dr Alan Huggins, Deputy Secretary, and David Bowles, Vice-Provost. The first edition was designed in College in conjunction with Ron Hill, the then Publications Officer; now, twelve years later, it has been completely re-designed by Phil Bushell, Art Director of The Newpoint Publishing Company Limited, and we are very grateful to him, as to Georgina Sober and others at Newpoint.

For the new index, we are much obliged to Murray Watson, the former Secretary of the Slade.

We have received valuable assistance from Mrs Janet Percival and Gill Furlong of the Library, Mrs E. F. Foster and Elizabeth Gibson of the Records Office and Mrs Mary Lightbown, Curator of the College Art Collection. E. E. Hitchcock, P. E. Harrison and the staff in the Central Photographic Unit photographed the bulk of the material used, often working from intractable sources. W. R. Merrington, the historian of the Hospital and the Medical School, kindly loaned a number of photographs. A. T. Picton, former Librarian of University College Hospital Medical School, also provided assistance, as did J. Cresswell of the Department of Chemistry, Mrs P. Karet of University College School, J. Prendergast of the National Portrait Gallery and J. Creasey of Dr Williams's Library. Nazneen Razwi, Secretary of the Department of History, and Kitty Stubbs, undertook typing with speed and efficiency. Tim Aspden of the Department of Geography drew the graph and the chart on p.231 and the map on p.237. We are indebted to them all.

We are grateful for information of various sorts provided by: L. J. Gue, the former Deputy Secretary; H. W. Callaghan, the former Deputy Librarian; A. J. L. Cahill, the former Registrar; J. W. Arterton, the present Registrar; R. Blackaby, former Assistant Secretary (Service and Establishments); E. Williamson, the former Bursar; H. J. W. Feasey formerly of the Personnel Division. We have drawn on the help of many of our academic colleagues, especially of the following: M. G. Ashby (Phonetics and Linguistics), K. B. Atkinson (Photogrammetry and Surveying), Dr Amelia Banks (Psychology), the late Professor H. E. M. Barlow (Electronic and Electrical Engineering), Mrs Lis-Anne Bawden (Slade), the late Professor R. E. D. Bishop (Mechanical Engineering), Professor F. W. Bullock (Physics and Astronomy), Professor A. R. Burgess (Chemical and Biochemical Engineering), Professor J. H. Burns (History), Professor G. Burnstock (Anatomy), Dr W. F. Bynum (History of Medicine), Dr F. W. Carter (Geography), Professor I. R. Christie (History), Professor H. D. Clout (Geography), the late Professor Sir William Coldstream (Slade), Dr D. A. Coleman (Anthropology), Professor A. L. Cullen (Electronic and Electrical Engineering), Professor J. S. Cummins (Spanish), Dr D. L. d'Avray (History), the late Dr C. Dodd (Physics and Astronomy), the late Professor J. M. Dodgson (English), Professor D. T. Donovan (Geology), Miss Jean Edmiston (Human Genetics and Biometry), Dr Kay Flavell

(German), J. A. Forty (Bartlett School), Professor A. J. Fourcin (Phonetics and Linguistics), Dr J. W. Fox (Physics and Astronomy), Dr A. M. Foyle (Bartlett School) the late R. B. Freeman (Zoology), Professor S. Greenbaum and B. D. Greenslade (English), Dr T. H. Gretton (History of Art), A.H. Griffiths (Latin and Greek) the late Dr G. Hall (French), Professor E.W. Handley (Greek), Mrs Margaret Harkness (Physiology), Professor F. F. Heymann (Physics and Astronomy), Professor J.I. Israel (History), Professor K. J. Ives (Civil and Municipal Engineering), Dr A. R. Jonckheere (Psychology), Dr P. H. Kemp (Civil and Municipal Engineering), G. E. Kenshole (Electronic and Electrical Engineering), Dr C. D. King (French), A. D. E. Lewis (Laws), J. M. A. Lindon (Italian), Professor A. Maccoll (Chemistry), Dr D. McNally (Physics and Astronomy), T. D. McFarland (German), Dr Pauline M. Meadow (Biochemistry), Dr Maxine P. M. Merrington (Statistics), A. J. Metheringham and Dr D. J. Miller (Physics and Astronomy), Professor A. W. Nienow (Chemical and Biochemical Engineering), Professor Sir Randolph Quirk (English), Professor P. A. Samet (Computer Centre), Dr W. A. Smeaton (History and Philosophy of Science), Dr A. C. H. Smith (Physics and Astronomy), Professor H. S. Smith (Egyptology), Jean Spencer (Slade), the late Professor J. A. C. Thomas (Laws), Professor A. G. Watson (Library, Archive and Information Studies), Helen D. Weston (History of Art), Dr D. J. B. White (Botany), and Professor Richard Wollheim (Philosophy).

Fellows of the College who provided assistance include the late Sir Thomas Cash, Professor Sir Harold Himsworth, Master I. H. Jacob, Professor R. A. Kekwick, the late Professor G. F. Marrian, A. Taylor Milne (who provided the quotation on p.33 from Selina Macaulay's unpublished diary, now in the Huntington Library, California), Dr K. P. Oakley, the late Professor Sir Alan Parkes, Sir John Rothenstein, Sir John Summerson, Sir Frederick Warner and Lord Zuckerman. Others who have provided information or assistance in a variety of ways include: M. L. Freeman, the Union Administrator; Bob Tivey, the former Administration and Finance Officer of the Union; Phil Wainwright, former Co-Editor of *Pi*; Barbara Adams of the Department of Egyptology; Mrs R. Down of the Zoology Museum; C. A. N. Evans of the Department of Physiology; Cathy Giangrande of the Institute of Archaeology; Claire Gobbi formerly of the Bentham Project; Dr B. A. Harwood formerly of the Registrar's Department; Dr C. J. Lucas, the former Director of the Health Centre; Wolfgang Klär, formerly the College's Typographical Adviser; J. M. Watson, the former Secretary of the Slade School; Jossi Balanescu of the Audio Visual Unit; I. W. G. Martin of the Library; the late Muriel Hopley of the Publications Department; Ian Wintersgill and Patricia Reynolds of Music Society; Jon Davies of Film Society and Mike Maltby, the Residence Officer.

Our debt to the previous historians of the College is so great as to amount at times to plagiarism. A particularly heavy debt is owed to H. Hale Bellot's scholarly and massive *University College London, 1826-1926* (1929). We have also made use of the writings of Henry Morley, R. W. Chambers, W. P. Ker, Carey Foster, F. W. Felkin and the lectures given by Norman Collie, Ernest Starling and others on the occasion of the Cententary in 1927, as well as more recent publications, especially David Taylor's *Godless Students of Gower Street* (1968) and W. R. Merrington's *University College Hospital and its Medical School: A History* (1976). For the second edition, Negley Harte's *The University of London, 1836-1986: An Illustrated History* (1986) has been available. We have foregone footnote references; the authority for virtually all the information contained in this book is to be found either in the publications mentioned or amongst the Library's admirable College Collection, the archives and records of which we have plundered but by no means exhausted.

The majority of the illustrations come from this source too, supplemented by our selection of material from the College Art Collection, the Records Office, the Publications Department, the Union and the Senior Common Room. Material was also culled from a number of academic Departments, particularly from Chemistry, Physics and Astronomy, the Slade, Physiology, Human Genetics and Biometry, Phonetics and Linguistics, Zoology, Egyptology, Psychology, Mechanical Engineering, Civil and Municipal Engineering, History, and French. Full acknowledgement of the source of all the illustrations used is gratefully given below.

Our final thanks go to Eva Harte and Helen Weston for their continuing forebearance and support.

SOURCES OF ILLUSTRATIONS

1. Hunting Aerofilms
2. UCL College Art Collection
3. UCL Central Photographic Unit
4. UCL Library, Bentham MSS
5. UCL Library, College Collection
6. National Portrait Gallery
7. Bonn University Library
8. Virginia University Library
9. Edinburgh University Library
10. UCL Library, College Archives
11. UCL College Art Collection
12. UCL Library, College Archives
13. A. Bain, James Mill: A Biography (1882)
14. Lady Knutsford, Life and Letters of Zachary Macaulay (1900)
15. Mrs. Grote, The Personal Life of George Grote (1873)
16. Dept of Chemistry
17. UCL College Art Collection
18. UCL Library, College Archives
19. UCL Library, Librarian's Room
20. Illustrated London News, 1863
21. UCL College Art Collection
22-23. UCL Library, College Archives
24. UCL Records Office, University College London, History of Faculty of Engineering
25-26. UCL Library, College Archives
27. National Portrait Gallery, 648
28-30. UCL Library, College Archives
31. Fitzwilliam Museum, Cambridge; on loan from the Master and Fellows of Trinity College, Cambridge
32. UCL Library, College Archives
33. National Portrait Gallery, 12399
34. Victoria and Albert Museum, Dept of Prints
35. UCL College Art Collection
36. Guildhall Library
37. Collection of N.B. Harte
38. UCL College Art Collection
39. UCL Library, College Archives
40-41. UCL Library, College Collection
42. British Museum, Dept of Prints and Drawings
43. UCL Library, College Archives
44. National Portrait Gallery, 446a
45. Courtesy of Dr W.R. Merrington
46-48. UCL Library, College Collection
49. Dept of Physics
50. UCL Library, College Archives
51. UCL Library, College Collection
52. Dept of Chemistry
53. Dept of Biology
54. National Portrait Gallery, 1010
55. Courtesy of Professor J.S. Cummins
56. UCL Library, College Collection
57. Courtesy of the Archivist, Brighton College
58. Faculty of Laws
59. UCL Library, College Archives
60. National Portrait Gallery, 677
61. British Museum, Dept of Oriental Printed Books
62. UCL College Art Collection
63. UCL Library, College Archives

64. National Portrait Gallery of Scotland
65. KCL Library
66. UCL Records Office
67. UCL Library, College Collection
68-70. UCL Library, College Archives
71-72. UCL College Art Collection
73-74. UCL Library, College Archives
75. Geographical Journal, 1960
76. UCL Library, College Collection
77. British Museum, Dept of Prints and Drawings
78. Dept of Physiology
79. UCL Library, College Collection
80. British Museum, Dept of Prints and Drawings
81. UCL Library, College Collection
82. UCL College Art Collection
83-86. UCL Library, College Collection
87. Illustrated London News, 1846
88. Courtesy of Dr W.R. Merrington
89. UCL Library, College Collection
90. Dr Williams' Library
91. UCL Library, College Collection
92. UCL Library, College Archives
93. Courtesy of Dr W.R. Merrington
94. Wellcome Institute of the History of Medicine
95. UCL Publications Dept
96. UCL College Art Collection
97. Punch, 1847
98. Pictorial Times, 1843
99. UCL Library, MS ADD 81/2
100. Dept of Physics
101. Thomas Sadler ed., Diary, Reminiscences and Correspondance of H.C. Robinson (1869)
102. UCL Library, College Collection
103. UCL Library, College Archives
104-6. UCL College Art Collection
107. UCL Library, College Collection
108. Dept of Geology
109. Courtesy of Dr W.R. Merrington
110-12. UCL College Art Collection
113-15. F.W. Felkin, From Gower Street to Frognal (1909)
116. Illustrated London News, 20 July 1878
117. Building News, 10 September 1880
118-19. UCL College Art Collection
120. UCL Library, College Collection
121. H.S. Solly, The Life of Henry Morley (1898)
122. Building News, 17 June 1881
123. Dept of Chemistry
124. University of Glasgow, Archives.
125. Courtesy of A.D.E. Lewis
126. Collection of Dr J.A. North.
127-29. Dept of Physics
130. UCL Library, College Collection
131. UCL Library, College Archives
132-34. UCL Library, College Collection
135. Courtesy of Mrs Rosina Down
136. UCL Library, College Collection
137. Dept of Biology
138-39. UCL Library, College Collection
140. Royal Society

141-44. UCL Library, College Collection
145-46. Courtesy of the late Professor R.E.D. Bishop.
147. Courtesy of Professor K.J. Ives.
148. Courtesy of Dr P.H. Kemp.
149. UCL College Art Collection
150. UCL Records Office, University College London, History of Faculty of Engineering
151. Courtesy of the late Professor H.E.M. Barlow
152. Dept of Geology
153-54. Courtesy of the late Professor H.E.M. Barlow
155. UCL Records Office
156-57. Courtesy of Professor K.J. Ives
158-61. Dept of Chemistry
162. Sphere, 23 July 1921.
163. Courtesy of Dr W.R. Merrington
164. UCL Library, Pearson MS
165. Galton Laboratory
166. UCL Library, Pearson MS
167. K. Pearson, The Life, Letters and Labours of Francis Galton, vol. III A (1930)
168-69. Galton Laboratory.
170-71. UCL Library, College Collection
172. UCL Library, College Archives
173-75. UCL Library, College Collection
176. Dept of Chemistry
177. UCL Library, College Collection
178. UCL Library, MS Misc
179. UCL Library, College Collection
180-85. Slade School
186-87. UCL College Art Collection
188. Slade School
189. UCL College Art Collection
190-94. Slade School
195. Institute of Classical Studies
196. UCL Library, College Collection
197. Sphere, 23 July 1921
198-200. Dept of Egyptology
201. UCL Records Office
202-3. UCL College Art Collection
204-5. UCL Library, College Collection
206-7. Courtesy of Dr W.R. Merrington
208. UCL Library, College Collection
209. Courtesy of Dr W.R. Merrington
210. Sir Rickman Godlee, The Past, Present and Future of the School for Advanced Medical Studies of University College London (1906)
211. UCL Library, College Collection
212. Courtesy of Dr W.R. Merrington
213. André Deutsch Ltd.
214. UCL Library, College Collection, Thane MS
215. Courtesy of Dr W.R. Merrington
216. UCL Records Office
217. UCL Library, College Collection
218. Windsor Magazine, 234 (1914)
219-22. UCL Union
223-29. UCL Library, College Collection
230. Dept of Physics
231. Journal of the Royal Institute of British Architects, March 1894
232. UCL Library, College Collection
233. UCL College Art Collection
234. UCL Records Office

INDEX